Good Naked

GOOD

JONI B. COLE

UNIVERSITY PRESS OF NEW ENGLAND

NAKED

*Reflections on
How to Write More,
Write Better, and
Be Happier*

HANOVER AND LONDON

University Press of New England
www.upne.com
© 2017 Joni B. Cole
All rights reserved
Manufactured in the United States of America
Typeset in Whitman by Passumpsic Publishing
Illustrations by Helmut Baer

Note: Some names of individuals and identifying features of stories in this book have been changed to maintain privacy.

For permission to reproduce any of the material in this book, contact Permissions, University Press of New England, One Court Street, Suite 250, Lebanon NH 03766; or visit www.upne.com

Paperback ISBN: 978-1-61168-911-2
Ebook ISBN: 978-1-5126-0054-4

Library of Congress Cataloging-in-Publication Data available on request

5 4 3 2 1

TO ESME,
who makes the world better by being Esme

TO THEA,
my role model for following your heart

Contents

Preface

Cheerleader for Mediocrity

As a creative writing instructor, I think I am good at my job, with the exception of two aspects: time management, and stopping people from going on and on in a workshop. Mostly, that second failing refers to me. I can get carried away when it comes to issues of narrative craft and what writers are capable of doing with their words. How can you not get excited? As writers, we can transport readers to wherever we want to take them. We can make people feel deeply, think new thoughts, forget about their troubles, and want to become better human beings, even while they are still in their bathrobes. We can change the world, and all it takes is the right word choice, syntax, and who knows how many drafts.

I have been happily teaching fiction and creative nonfiction writing to adults for twenty years. By now, my guess is that at least 1,000 people in my small town have taken one of my workshops, or so I tell myself to feel better when I forget a former participant's name. My teaching career started when I was working as an editor at a regional magazine and offered a creative writing workshop out of my office. The evening of that first class, one participant made quite the entrance, arriving fifteen minutes late in a fur coat and heels. This was March in Vermont, mud season, which is also sugaring season. The woman took a seat in the circle of chairs next to another woman in overalls and spattered boots, who had come directly to class after spending the day tapping maple trees. In a world marred by so much contentiousness and polarity, the image of those two writers, side by side, thoughtfully critiquing each other's manuscripts, still gives me hope for a more tolerant, united tomorrow.

After I quit the magazine job, I moved my teaching practice to a back room of my old, big-hearted house, where I continued to run workshops for about ten years, during which time our household grew, first through the adoption of an incontinent dog, and eventually with the arrival of one baby girl, then another daughter born two years later. Because of the dog's medical issue, my family was disinclined to own carpets, hence I can remember so many Thursday evening meetings punctuated by the sound of my little girls playing jacks upstairs on the hardwood floor, while beneath them writers discussed characterization, plot, and our various writing-related neuroses.

Over time, I began teaching in MFA programs, at literary conferences, and, more recently, through social service agencies. I also opened my own writer's center in a building on Main Street, aptly named Dreamland. Compared to other writer's centers around the country that have staffs and host an impressive diversity of programs and events, mine is small in size, but not in heart or literary integrity. We gather to do good work, in a room with orange walls and mismatched chairs that the group members claim with an inordinate degree of proprietariness. The other evening, a former participant from over a year ago rejoined the workshop, and told the man already settled in the green velvet chair with the sunken cushion that this was *her* seat. She tried to pretend she was kidding. That quirk alone makes me find writers refreshingly odd and good company. How could anyone not want to hang out with us?

On the other hand . . .

"I hate writing. I love having written." This comment is most often attributed to the witty author, poet, and critic Dorothy Parker, but I also could attribute it to any number of my writer friends and workshop participants because, let's face it, a lot of us are in the habit of *bemoaning*. But what I found particularly unsettling several years ago was when I heard that statement coming from my own mouth. What? I hate writing? Was this really how

I felt? If so, then why had I chosen to be a writer? Why did I devote so many hours, and so much energy, to doing something that did not make me happy? In hindsight, I am pretty sure that unguarded comment—at once revelatory and disturbing—seeded the idea for this book.

In my workshops, I do not ask to read writing samples before allowing newcomers to join a group. I let everyone in, and mix us all up—newbies, authors with contracts, writers of fantasy and thrillers, memoirists, essayists, local literary luminaries, even people who bring their knitting to class, though that last category demands a good deal of my patience. A lot of participants are initially suspicious of this kind of democratization. ("I don't want to be in a group with a bunch of amateurs." "I don't want to be in a group where everyone is better than me!") Whatever. Everyone usually comes around. Our method in class is to meet every manuscript at whatever stage it has arrived in the creative process, and to kindly help usher it along toward the next draft. In this measured way, we manage to cover all aspects of narrative technique, without having the writer's head implode.

Despite the differences in our genres, experience levels, and talents, I have come to recognize that most writers—including those inside and outside workshops—share certain sensibilities. One notable example: we seem to do better when we are cheered on along the way, particularly because most of us are lousy at doing this for ourselves. We have a tendency to doubt our abilities and to show disdain for our drafts, especially if we write too long in isolation. That is yet another reason for my enthusiasm in a workshop—it addresses a deficit, and plays an important role in any educational interaction. Please note that when I say enthusiasm, my connotation is derived from Late Latin: *enthusiasmus*, meaning divinely inspired, as in possessed by a god. I like the sound of that.

Of course, not everyone sees it the same way.

"A cheerleader for mediocrity." That is how a good friend and workshop participant described me one evening over drinks after class. I cannot remember the particular stories the group had discussed earlier that evening, but I suspect they must have needed a great deal of work, which only would have made me more determinedly upbeat. *A cheerleader for mediocrity.* I tried to laugh off the comment; it is, after all, a clever line, and that counts for a lot in my social circle. But mediocrity? Are you kidding me? As a teacher, I am the last person to say good is good enough. Just the other day, I returned to a seasoned writer a manuscript covered with notes penned in my nearly illegible scrawl.

"Oh my." He looked surprised, and not in a good way. "I had thought it was perfect."

"It is perfect," I reassured him. "Perfect for this draft. And now it's time to move on to the next draft."

This man was writing for publication, but even if a person says to me something to the effect that "I'm just writing for my grandkids," my critique would be equally uncompromising. Say this doting grandparent had written the following sentence: *I put my head on the desk and rested.*

"Come now," I would respond, "imagine if your little grandchildren came across that passage and thought Nana had actually detached her own head, and set it down on a piece of furniture. That would be awfully traumatic for a young person, don't you think? How about you have another go at it?"

So, what was I missing? How did a teacher like me, with my relentless call for revision (not to mention my talent for divine inspiration), translate to a cheerleader for mediocrity?

Cognitive science tells us that if you do not understand the flaws in a person's reasoning, you are not going to be able to dislodge his or her misconceptions and replace them with correct concepts. Motivated by this insight, I think I have finally figured out the flaw in my friend's reasoning, which is the same wrong thinking a lot of us buy into—that mediocre writing is a sign of failure. In fact, mediocre writing is a normal, productive part of the creative process, the precursor to quality writing, and therefore, I believe, it merits a good bit of cheering on. You cannot spend as many years as I have in the company of writers, and this includes myself, and not become aware of certain tics, behaviors, and misconceptions we tend to share that do not make any sense, and do not do us any favors. This tendency to disparage works-in-progress—our own, as well as those shared by others seeking guidance—reflects just one way that writers and writing instructors can be wrong, even when we are so sure that we are right.

Maybe because I live in Vermont, I see a lot of cars sporting Ben and Jerry's bumper stickers that read, *If it's not fun, why do it?* I am big on fun. In fact, I am one of the most fun people I know, though I suspect some former co-workers and relatives might disagree. Regardless, that bumper sticker has always bothered me. I do not think fun should be the arbiter of everything we do. ("Sorry, honey, but helping out around the house is kind of a drag, so I'm gonna have to cut out.") So I do not have a problem reconciling my life's work with the fact that it is not always fun, but what I cannot reconcile is a life spent doing work that makes me miserable a good part of the time. I want my writing to have meaning, and I want to find meaning in the act of writing. For me, this has to include feelings of well-being, satisfaction, pride, and gratitude throughout the creative process. In short, I want to experience happiness in the deepest sense when I write, even when I am struggling on the page, even when I am confronting painful subjects.

I wrote this book because I want writers, including myself, to cheer up. I want us to swap out the all-too-common mindsets and practices that do not serve us for ones that feed our creativity, our productivity, and our souls. A lot of us attribute our artistic failures and frustrations to forces outside ourselves, when most of the time we are the ones who get in our own way. After twenty years of teaching, I have witnessed this phenomenon countless times, but I also have seen how the concepts shared on these pages have helped novices, seasoned authors, and even knitters enjoy more informed, inspired, and joyful writing lives. What surprised me, however, was that it was not until I was actually working on this book that I applied these same concepts so diligently to my own creative life.

Writing is a discovery process, and what I discovered when I attended to my own tics, behaviors, and misconceptions was a much more positive writing practice. I can now let go of my worry that I was devoting so many hours, and so much energy, to a journey that offered few rewards until it was complete. I can now write more, write better, and be happier along the way. Of course, I still catch myself bemoaning on occasion; bad habits die hard, and a writer's nature is what it is. But what I can say now that I could not say before is this—I like the fact that I have written, and I like to write, at least most of the time.

Happiness is one of those concepts that neither needs, nor conforms to, a formal definition. You just know it when you feel it. Ideally, the concepts in these pages will make you want to bound to your desk, whistling in anticipation of the work ahead, and never have a bad writing day again. Short of that, my goal with this book is to help you cultivate your own form of happiness as you engage in your creative work.

"Give me a W! R! I! T! E!"

You get the idea. I sincerely hope that the words that follow serve to cheer you on.

PLANET WRITER

"Do NOT put me in your book!"

First Things First (Not)

You have a Great Idea for a story. You are so infatuated with this Great Idea that you gush to your friends and fellow writers—"I'm going to write a book about [insert your Great Idea here]!" Your Great Idea takes up residence in your psyche. It settles in, as entitled and undisciplined as lesser royalty. Weeks pass, then months, but nothing gets written. Your Great Idea begins to pace the shag carpet of your mind.

"What's the holdup, hon?" your Great Idea asks. "These shoes are killing me."

"I just need a little more time," you tell your Great Idea. "I'm not sure how to get started."

Life continues, crowding the inside of your head with more experiences, more people, more memories, more distractions: *Ticks! When's the last time I checked myself for ticks?* Still, even with so much going on in your world, you keep revisiting your Great Idea in your mind. By now, its shoes are off. Its feet rest on the coffee table of your consciousness, next to a highball sweating on the once burnished cherry tabletop. You think, *Why can't it use a coaster?*

"I thought you loved me," your Great Idea nags. "I thought you were all, like, I want to spend time with you. You mean so much to me. I want us to have a future together."

And your Great Idea is right. You did want that. You still want that. You loved your Great Idea then and you love it now, only now it is starting to feel more like a love-hate relationship because you cannot think about your Great Idea without feeling guilty. *I'm just too busy to sit down and write*, you tell yourself, citing your dependents, the crumbs in your bread drawer, your commitment to world peace. Deep down, however, you know it is not family, or work, or even your ideal of planetary nonviolence that is keeping you away from your desk. This editorial paralysis is all about your fear of making a wrong first move. This is the real reason you cannot commit to your Great Idea.

Where to start? Where to start?

"What is it with you artist types?" Your Great Idea shrugs away your latest excuse, and returns its attention to the crossword. This is not a puzzle from the *New York Times*, you notice, but one with a picture of a TV celebrity in the center of the grid. "Vanna!" you hear yourself screaming. "The five-letter name of a 'Lucky Letter Turner' is Vanna. Even an imbecile knows that!" But what really upsets you is how your Great Idea made air quotes when it said the word "artist."

A year, then another, passes.

"Whatever happened to your Great Idea?" If one more friend asks you this, you will instantly unfriend them. Why can't people mind their own beeswax? You bite open your third snack pack of smoked almonds. How is this even possible, that seventeen little almonds could add up to 100 calories?

Where to start? Where to start?

Finally, maybe because your youngest is packing for his gap year in Carmel, or you read on Facebook that your high school class is planning its thirtieth reunion, or you simply cannot *not* write any longer, you plant yourself at your desk, determined to stay put until you eke out a first paragraph. But years of neglect have taken their toll. Your once beautiful Great Idea now seems to bear the features of a feral pig. Its back bristles at your approach. Malice glints from its slivered eyes. For a moment, you worry it may have been to blame for your neighbor's short hair going missing. That is how bad things have become in your head.

Where to start? Where to start?

Despite your resolve, you still cannot commit to a keystroke. What if you begin here when you should begin there? What if you write down this idea, no, that idea, but then another idea comes along that might be even better? And if you set off in the wrong direction, how long will it take you to find your way back? I understand this panicky feeling because one time a friend and I had tickets to fly to Los Angeles out of the Manchester, New Hampshire, airport, but we ended up at the airport in Hartford, Connecticut, all because we got on the wrong highway a mere ten minutes into the trip. Now that was a logistical nightmare.

Where to start? Where to start?

Your neck muscles ratchet into a double helix. You want to cry. You do cry, and then you go to the mirror to see what you look like when you are crying. You are a wreck, and looking old, so much older than when you first thought of writing a story about your Great Idea. And yet, even after all this time, one thing relentlessly remains the same. You do not know where to start, so you cannot get started.

If this scenario sounds at all familiar, you do indeed have a problem. Only it is not the problem you think you have. When launching a novel or memoir—or any creative work for that matter—the issue isn't that you don't have a clue where your story should start; the issue is that you think you should have a clue, even before you start writing.

I know so many writers who have carried around their book ideas for years.

"I've wanted to write about my mother's immigration experience ever since she died in 1973."

"My goal was to write a travel book about my bike trip across Europe, but now it seems like ancient history."

"Ever since college, I've wanted to write a novel about a funeral director who lives on a houseboat, but I never knew the best way to begin."

I am sure these people felt buoyant when their story ideas first struck them, but even a one-pound hand weight can drag you down if you lug it around long enough.

If you are like most writers, and by most writers I mean all but four, the perfect opening for your story will never manifest in your mind. Yes, there is always that one author we have all encountered at a book signing or writing conference who points to his receding hairline and explains to his rapt audience, "I write it all up here, and then just put it down on the page." We can admire this author and wish we were like him, perhaps with more hair, but know that this fellow is the exception to the rule, and perhaps not to be completely trusted. Typically, the creative process needs more than a head to sort itself out. Thus, thinking you need to figure out chapter one (or even more distressing, first figure out your preface, then your introduction, and then chapter one) before you start typing away will only succeed in eating up a lot of time, and will make you feel constipated and grouchy. The good news, however, is that these bad feelings are also what push a lot of people past their resistance to join a writing workshop, which is at least one productive thing that can come from such misguided thinking. I know my classes certainly attract people struggling with this issue, including Lynne, a professional feature writer who knows her way around a page. Regardless, when Lynne got an idea for a mystery novel about a woman whose teenaged son goes missing after soccer practice, she spent months feeling stuck because she didn't know where to begin her narrative.

"I have a sense of what I want to happen, but I just can't figure out the first scene," Lynne told our group.

"So forget about the first scene," I advised. "Write any scene you feel fairly certain belongs somewhere in the story. Even better, write the rescue scene where the missing son is discovered alive and well!" I offered this last suggestion because I have little tolerance for authors who kill off children or pets, even if these plot points are in service to the story. Having worked with so many aspiring authors like Lynne—who have gone on to complete powerful stories by following this same advice to start anywhere—I knew this was excellent counsel, from my perspective a no-brainer. But maybe because it is a no-brainer, literally, in that we need to temporarily disengage our brains from its insistence on first things first, this concept is often met with resistance.

But I can't just start anywhere. It feels so loosey-goosey!

I will assume you are thinking this because most people respond to this advice in a similar fashion, at least until they try it. As writers, we may be described as creative types, but that does not mean we don't like feeling in control, or crave the comfort of structure and predictability as much as the next guy. Human nature does not step easily into the unknown, especially if we think it will cause us more work.

But my book needs a proper beginning!

What book? At the moment, all you have is a feral pig. Perhaps that last comment was unnecessarily harsh, but so many writers tend to try to reduce the creative process to a linear equation because they think that is the proper way to proceed. *Listen Great Idea, you are not leaving this head until you tell me where to start!* Would that you and your Great Idea could cuddle up in your consciousness together, figure it all out, and then step out onto the page accompanied by a herald of Hallelujahs. No rings on the tabletop. No mess. But messes, you might want to remind yourself, can be fun. They can be the stuff of inspiration. And the reality is, even if the "perfect" opening for your Great Idea does present itself in your mind, it is just as likely to be a false start. By this, I mean that, more often than not, where you think you should start your narrative will actually end up being better suited as backstory embedded in a later chapter. Just sayin'.

Where to start? Where to start?

Shush. Of course, in the end, your narrative needs to open with exactly the right scene, and by exactly the right scene I mean exactly the right scene. For that matter, all the scenes, from the first to the last, must contribute to a flow that establishes not just a chronology but a causality that drives the plot forward and makes readers curious, if not frantic, to know what happens next. Still, none of that needs to be figured out at the front end of writing. And the future structure of your manuscript will not suffer one iota by not writing it from the beginning to the end. In fact, quite the opposite. Starting the creative process anywhere allows you to jump right in to a scene, any scene, that demands your attention. Recall Lynne, the stuck writer who had an idea for a mystery but could not figure out her opening. Week two of the workshop, she returned with a scene that takes place well after the protagonist's son disappears, when the town is in the midst of a community-wide search for the boy. Lynne knew this event would fall later in her narrative, but this was the scene that she wanted to write in the moment, partially because it was the one that felt the most vivid to her.

"It was like a revelation," Lynne shared, "that I didn't have to start writing on page one." And from there, she was on her way, racking up more scenes every week by working with, rather than against, her creative process.

But I don't want to waste time writing a jumble of scenes without any sense of order.

I imagine this is yet another concern on your mind, which I will counter by asking you this question: How much time have you already wasted not getting any of your Great Idea down on paper? If your answer is, say, six minutes or longer, then I would argue that writing something that might fall somewhere, anywhere, in your story is better than not writing your beginning, which may not even end up being your beginning.

But, but, but . . .

Honey, I think it is fair to say that both you and your Great Idea are looking a bit worse for wear. Plus, I am worried that your Great Idea is getting tired of waiting around for you, and just may take off at some point, leaving behind nothing but crumpled snack-pack wrappers and bitter memories. So please, stop fretting that you are not among those four writers who know exactly where to begin their stories before they actually start scribbling on the page. If it helps, know that those four writers are creative freaks, and everyone is afraid to talk to them, even their moms. The time has come to forget about finding the perfect opening to your novel or memoir or whatever, and simply dive in.

But, but . . .

Shush! I'm sorry to keep shushing you because I know from personal experience how annoying that can be, but you need to quiet your mind and listen to the following good news. I have come up with the perfect writing exercise for people in your predicament! In fact, if you use this prompt to begin your work, I am certain that you will launch your story in the best way possible, and your relationship with your Great Idea will be restored to what it was before both of you did things that you would rather forget.

But . . .

"Goodbye. I'll miss you." There you go. That is the perfect writing prompt for you, guaranteed. "Goodbye, I'll miss you." Just put those words on the page, then keep writing, capturing whatever flows through your fingertips to your keyboard or pen. Write without judgment, or second-guessing, or thinking. Write without worrying about beginnings, middles, or endings. Write now. Right now.

How do I know this is the perfect exercise to launch your particular Great Idea? I know because it is the same for every writer who has ever felt stuck before even getting started. When it comes to beginnings, saying goodbye is as good a way as any to send us off on our merry way.

Planet Writer

I have often thought, if I wasn't a writer and writing instructor, I would like to be a cultural anthropologist. I think I have a proclivity for this kind of scholarship, and not just because I like digging through other people's medicine cabinets to sample their beauty products and make assumptions based on their prescription pill bottles. I have always been curious about humans and why they act and think the way they do. How does a group or society organize and govern itself? What is its belief system? Why are certain practices deigned normal and acceptable within a specific culture, even if—at least from an outsider's perspective— they run counter to reality, productivity, and well-being?

For over twenty years, I have paid particular attention to one group of people, that is, my people, those of us who reside on what I call Planet Writer. Although the inhabitants of Planet Writer are not bound by a particular geography, we nevertheless exhibit a distinct mindset and distinct behaviors. On Planet Writer, for example, we dwell in a culture that esteems language and devotes considerable, sometimes excruciating, attention to its nuance, rhythm, presentation, and power. In other words, we love words! Though sometimes they drive us crazy. Consider the following quote by the poet Edwin Arlington Robinson, winner of three Pulitzer Prizes: "This morning I took the hyphen out of Hell-hound . . . and this afternoon I put it back."

Ours also is a culture that places great value on the importance of sharing stories as a means of edification, entertainment, and activism. This is why we devote countless hours to committing our life experiences or fictional works to the page. In our heads is a recurring volley of emotions: I have something to say! No I don't! I love writing! Writing sucks! Yet, despite the doubts, we continue to be drawn to our desks. This labor of love-slash-argh feeds something inside us that no other avocation or vocation can nourish as effectively. I have a friend who is a financial planner. He helps seniors hold on to their life's savings so they can keep their homes and afford long-term care. What could be more important? He is also the author of several detective novels, which he publishes through Amazon. Here is what he said to me the other day over a plate of sushi: "If only I could give up my day job and write full time, now that would feel rewarding."

Our respect for language, our creativity, our need to share stories real and imagined—these traits serve to make Planet Writer a most meaningful place to dwell. Of course, we share other beliefs and practices on a less lofty level. For instance, we often put great stock in rituals, performing ceremonies in prescribed ways as a means of protection from the dark force, aka writer's block. Though these rituals are highly personalized, some examples might include "lighting" the flameless candle on our desk, even during broad daylight, or drinking sixty-four fluid ounces of decaf ginger peach tea throughout the day. For the latter, the type of mug is of particular significance, and must be just so in terms of shape and grip. Equally important is what the mug evokes, whether it is a souvenir reminder of your first trip to England (where you decided to name your main character Nigel!) or that special Mother's Day gift your teenager bought you from Dollar Tree.

As a people, writers also have a preternatural gift for manufacturing lively internal monologues, as in, *Why can't my kid cough up the money for a nicer gift? And what if this dollar-store mug isn't microwaveable, and every time I reheat my Cup-a-Soup, I'm ingesting toxic chemicals?* To self-soothe, we have developed a variety of comfort practices. At home, we often prefer to stay in our pajamas as long as possible, and our stance on showering can be quite liberal, at least when we are under deadline. If we join a workshop, we usually try to sit in the same seat every week. In addition, while we are an educated people, more than capable of understanding the concept of a living wage, few things mean more to us than acceptance from a publisher, even after we are told that, in exchange for our work, we will be paid only in copies.

Okay, so Planet Writer is not perfect. But this is why I think it behooves us to take a more anthropological view of the culture that shapes our creative lives. What beliefs and practices do we just buy into because, well, just because?

Consider one of the most pervasive, yet spurious convictions within our culture—the myth of the suffering artist. A general understanding among creative types is that misery feeds our work. Aristotle may have been the first to spread this rumor when he wrote, "All men who have attained excellence in philosophy, in poetry, in art and in politics . . . had a melancholic habitus." Seriously, Aristotle? We must dwell in melancholy to create works of art? To me, such a "mandate" sounds more like an excuse for wallowing and bad behavior.

"Aristotle, dear," I can just hear his wife cajoling him in Ancient Greece, "when you get home from the Lyceum, would you mind watching the children for a bit so I can have some time to myself in the courtyard?"

"I'm sorry, Herpyllis," Aristotle replies. "I'm just too busy suffering for my art to pull my weight on the home front."

Thanks, Aristotle, for providing an excuse for centuries of self-absorbed artists to behave badly. But the myth of the suffering artist is not just an excuse for some creative types to justify moping and mood swings; it also can potentially subvert writers who are lovely people, people who do not relish clinging to misery, but worry that it is a prerequisite for inspiration. Here is just one example.

A much-published poet took a series of my writing workshops, after she decided she wanted to incorporate more narrative techniques into her work. Before and after class, I often would see her drafting her poems and stories at a nearby café, looking just how I wished I looked when hanging out at that same café—contemplative, immersed in a creative project, pretty in an adjunct professor type of way. The slim pillar of books she stacked near her notepad, whether for reference or to keep company with a few favorite authors, justified her solitary presence at a table for four.

The workshop, as usual, opened with introductions. "Tell us about your writing goals," I invited the circle of new and familiar faces. I am always comforted when former participants return for another class. It makes me think I must be doing something right. Plus, the presence of repeat participants helps reassure the newcomers that I am not one of those teachers who crush students' egos to test their worth as writers.

When it was the poet's turn to talk about her goals for the upcoming workshop, she was uncharacteristically hesitant. Her long bangs, cut at a sharp angle, bifurcated her face. This was a new look for her, one that made me like her all the more. Fashion-wise, floppy hair is more my taste, but geometric hairstyles tend to make for more unique characterization.

"I want to get started on another collection," the poet volunteered, "but I'm worried that I won't be able to write." An image of her recently updated Facebook photo flashed through my mind; it was a picture of her doing a cartwheel on a beach. *But you're my age*, I almost blurted, *and just look at what you can do!*

Instead, I asked, "Why in the world would you be worried? Every time I see you, you're scribbling away." And so it began again just minutes into a new class, the real work of my job as a teacher in the creative realm, to neither ignore, nor indulge, a student's insecurities.

"I'm in love," the poet confessed, looking dispirited. "I've never felt this happy in my whole life, so I'm worried I won't be able to write."

Oh, the ways we make our lives harder than they have to be. For perspective, imagine if an accountant confessed doubts about his ability to tally numbers, just because he found himself in a stable relationship. Or if an astronomer worried that, say, winning the lottery might rob her of her appreciation of the wonders of the night sky. One might argue that the work of an artist demands a more sensitive soul, but that sounds like elitism to me, as if by virtue of our calling our feelings run deeper than the rest of humanity. I would counter that we are all human. We all experience torment, and joy, and the heebie-jeebies for that matter. We may like to think the air on Planet Writer is more rarefied than in other realms, but I think it is both wrong and self-destructive to claim suffering as our particular birthright.

Of course, herein lies the confusion. As writers, unhappiness is what frequently drives us to write. When I conceived the idea for my This Day book series, I was feeling lower than I had ever felt in my life. My family had recently suffered a major loss. I was out of work. And I had just had a fight with my four-year-old daughter who refused to wear socks on a sleety, April day. Staring out my bedroom window, still in my pajamas past noon, I wondered if any other woman was feeling so low. Surely not. But what were other women doing and feeling and thinking on this very same day? That question—inspired by a pity party—was the seed of a book series that spanned three volumes, and involved the participation of thousands of women across the country, and from all walks of life.

In my workshops, I see so many stories, real and fictional, that were fueled by grief or painful personal experiences. We need to do justice to these feelings. We need to go to the crawl spaces in our minds to achieve authenticity on the page. Hence, even as you sit at your desk, frantically shaking your head and shouting silently, "Don't go in the basement!" the writer in you knows that is exactly where you must go. And so, you grab a flickering flashlight and creak, creak, creak down the cobwebby stairs of your mind, mining for misery in service to your story. Our characters must suffer to some degree because that is what drives them to action. That is what sets up the potential for a shift in their mental landscape, which constitutes a satisfying ending. Given this necessity, it would be fine if we bandied about the phrase "suffering protagonists," because that would remind us that, in stories, only trouble is interesting. Fortunately, however, we are not our protagonists. Suffering is not required for us to do our jobs. In fact, neuroscientists researching creativity have found that positive emotional states are actually better for concentration and productivity, and help steady the mind for a complexity of reasons. Of equal note, the release of dopamine, the chemical in your brain that makes you feel good, actually triggers creativity. In addition, studies have found that happy people make more money and live longer, which all seems to suggest that happiness does not have much of a downside.

And yet, the myth of the suffering artist and its alleged value to the creative process prevails, and it is not hard to figure out why. Many of the world's most famous writers were as noteworthy for their psychic pain as their literary gifts. Depression. Addiction. Mental illness. Because creative expression is an outlet for pain, this is likely why people who are battling emotional demons, or confronting life's cruelties, often gravitate toward artistic disciplines. I would hope all people in difficult circumstances avail themselves of the palliative powers of writing, whether in the form of journaling, personal narratives, or comic novels. It can demand an enormous amount of courage and stamina to create during times of trouble and when filled with despair. Thus, all the more reason to credit the person, not his afflictions or circumstances, for his creative work.

But who am I to tell you or anybody except myself to cheer up? Unless you have cornered me at a party and are endlessly bitching about your first-world problems, I would be out of line to suggest you stop your bellyaching and chillax. I also know that telling someone how she should feel usually has the reverse effect, similar to when I am just hanging around somewhere, minding my own business, and some stranger walks by and tells me to smile. *You smile, mother#@#!#!*, I think, even though, up until that point, I had been feeling quite even-tempered.

What I do think is fair advice, however, is this: Do not make a point to suffer. World-weariness does not have to be the writer's default. Do not be fearful that experiencing joy or a sense of well-being will risk your writing life. Hemingway once said, "Happiness in intelligent people is the rarest thing I know." I interpret these words to mean that anyone with half a brain can see that the world is screwed up, people can be hideous, and pandas are endangered. Knowing all this, how can we not feel miserable all the time? If my interpretation is accurate, then I want to say here, for the record, that I think Hemingway had it all wrong. I think that intelligence allows for a much broader perspective, one where we can acknowledge or even have firsthand experience with the existential void, but still find a way to reconcile the dark with the light, to bear witness to pain even while we live with hope.

It may be difficult to let go of the myth of the suffering artist. It may require years of therapy, or a sharp, figurative head-smack, given that this negative spin traces as far back as Ancient Greece. It may require falling in love, like that poet in my workshop, and then going on to write a critically acclaimed collection of prose poems about the joys of finding your soul mate. (Yes, that is what

actually happened.) So, in closing, I would like to offer this suggestion, one of particular use to writers, given how fond we are
of rituals. Light a candle. Not a flameless one this time, but a real
one. Take it outside, under sunny skies or beneath the moon. On
a piece of paper, write down the word "suffering." Use the candle
to set the paper on fire. Witness how this process of letting go of
pain releases light and warmth. Watch the ashes of your suffering
dance in the air, then drift to another planet far, far away.

The Writer from Vermont

Some time ago I was visiting my dad in the nursing home where he had lived since a stroke left him in need of skilled care. He was dozing in his recliner by the window, while I ate an extra brownie smuggled back from lunch and watched television. I hated that now my trips from Vermont to see my parents in Pennsylvania meant afternoons spent in the nursing home. I hated seeing my once funny, active dad so diminished, and my mom too worn down with anxiety about my dad to pay much attention to me. I hated how everything about my parents' lives had changed for the worse after my dad got sick, but I did love the excuse to sit in an overheated room, eating sweets, and watching mindless television all afternoon.

A woman wearing scrubs patterned with flamingos came into my dad's room. She had yellow hair with black roots, and a friendly demeanor.

I introduced myself, as she adjusted my dad's fleece blanket.

"Oh you're the youngest daughter!" My dad was sleeping, so she stage-whispered her enthusiasm. "You're the writer from Vermont!"

"Why, yes," I straightened in my dad's wheelchair, which I was using to sit closer to the television. How lovely that my reputation had preceded me.

The aide started bustling through her other care-giving duties.

The Writer from Vermont. My goodness, I liked the way that sounded. I pictured a woman sitting on the porch swing of her rustic farmhouse. Her view overlooks rolling, green fields. The mountains in the distance etch a brilliant blue sky. At her feet, her golden lab, Shi-Day (peace in Tibetan), gently snores. From a tray on the wicker side table, she helps herself to a slice of crusty bread she baked that very morning in the beehive oven in her fireplace. A cloth-covered journal rests in her lap. *The whisper song of the hermit thrush*, she pens, *so haunting, so beautiful* . . .

"Enjoy the rest of your visit." The aide snapped off her latex gloves and dumped them in the trash can by the door.

"Yes, you, too." Too late, I realized my response did not even make any sense.

I had planned to do some writing while sitting with my dad, but the effort seemed too much, so I escaped back into the made-for-TV movie I had been watching, though the clueless main character was seriously getting on my nerves. Why would an heiress marry a man, however dashing, who claims to work in the import-export business? Everyone knows those types of vaguely exotic professions are the preferred cover for psychopaths. The woman's family had warned her that he was only after her money, but she refused to listen. And now her new hubby was trying to kill her on their honeymoon! The heiress's limo careened down a treacherous road in the Alps. Surprise, surprise: brake failure. That is what you get, I thought, as I finished my last bite of brownie, when you only believe what you want to believe.

Isn't it interesting how other people's illusions can seem so obvious, and yet we can be completely convinced of our own willful misperceptions?

The Writer from Vermont. Technically speaking, I am that person, given that I write for a living and have lived in the Green Mountain State upwards of twenty years, which is long enough to almost not be considered a flatlander. But what I really want to believe is that I am the *romanticized* version of that person, the Writer from Vermont as she might be cast in a made-for-TV movie. In marketing, everyone knows that the Vermont label adds cachet to a brand, implying an association with wholesomeness, integrity, and cows. So, already I have that going for me. Even without the Vermont modifier, the term *writer* has its own elevated status, suggestive of someone who is deep, intelligent, creative. Or at least I like to think so. Even though I live in a condo overlooking a busy street, I want people to see me as that woman on the porch swing of her rustic farmhouse, surrounded by pastoral views, living the life of an artist. Can't you just hear the birdsong? Can't you just smell the cow droppings?

Writers are part of a cabal. Regardless of our diverse genres, our opposing political views, or even our rancorous disagreements over what defines "literary" fiction, we are all united in one common goal: maintaining the illusion that we are not like regular people. For example, recently I had a writing day where I bounced back and forth, from staring helplessly at my manuscript, to doing important chores, including shaking the toner cartridge. The next morning, in an email to a friend who is also working on a book, I whined about how little I had accomplished. My friend wrote back, "OMG. I didn't write ONE word yesterday. Must've been some kinda cosmic block." That is what I am talking about. Regular people can only blame a bad workday on the Internet crashing, or too much partying the night before, or incompetent co-workers. Writers, on the other hand, get to assign their success or failure to nothing less than the cosmos, or its creative ambassador, the muse.

But does this lofty view of ourselves do us any favors? In certain situations, yes, like when we are at our spouse's faculty party, holding a plate with a conspicuous heap of shrimp, while everyone around us guffaws at some esoteric joke about Indo-Russian trade relations. But what about when we are alone at our writing desks? What about when we are confronted with the reality that, oh my goodness, to be a writer requires that you actually have to write? In these situations, when you look into the cold glare of your computer screen, is it the face of the cosmos you see looking back at you in your moment of need? Is it a be-robed goddess waiting to sing you inspiration? Or is it just you, all by your lonesome, looking puffier than usual from overindulging in shellfish?

I would argue that the illusions we foster about ourselves as artists, and about the creative process, serve little practical purpose. In fact, they do us more harm than good. For starters, it is counterproductive, not to mention a bit nutty, that we talk about muses as if they are actually real. How is that different than believing in Santa Claus, and the possibility that this benevolent round man will squeeze down our chimney, leaving us presents, maybe a completed manuscript, a book contract, and an expert in social media already tweeting about our forthcoming release!

The downside of this kind of magical thinking, even if we only pay it lip service, is that it can negatively influence our behavior in very real ways. Yes, there are moments in the act of creation so inspired they may seem only attributable to divine intervention, but too much emphasis on creativity as a mystical experience means that we miss all sorts of opportunities to enhance our creative powers in more practical, earthly ways.

Researchers who have studied the creative process over decades have determined that creativity does not reside outside ourselves. Rather, it is an extension of what we already know. All behaviors and ideas are generative, building on the ones that came before. What this more realistic view of creativity means is that you are always in the flow—a word often associated with creativity.

Here is an example that demonstrates a typical writer in the flow, even when she herself believes that she is a victim of a cosmic block. Picture this typical writer doing what most writers do when they feel uncreative—she abandons her work to stare into the fridge. The door gapes open, wasting electricity. She spots an open container of shriveled cauliflower on the middle shelf. *Who puts leftovers in the fridge without covering them?* she asks herself.

You do, she answers, remembering that she lives alone, except for her four cats. She reaches down to pick up one of her pets, which jars a thought: the main character in her novel also lives alone. He should host a dinner party! He could invite the new tenant in apartment 12A; a young man whose fashion sense runs toward argyle sweater vests.

"Here, kitty, kitty! Here, Winslow!" Even as the typical writer stares into the fridge, she begins composing dialogue for her protagonist, having just decided that he also owns four cats, one of which is a Persian named Winslow whom he will take for walk in order to intercept 12A on the stairwell.

Now who is wasting electricity? Not the typical writer. Not you, if you are prone to staring into your fridge when the writing comes slow. As this example demonstrates, creativity flows from within as you react and respond to external stimuli, as one idea generates another. Indeed, the more diverse the stimuli the better, to move your thinking in fresh directions. This example also shows that creativity does not require evoking a muse, unless you consider shriveled cauliflower your muse, which actually makes sense. Your brain sees everything as inspiration. The generative mechanisms underlying the creative process are always at work, in both the right and the left cerebral hemispheres, which debunks another myth that creative people are "right-brained."

What this understanding means, however, is that we must pay attention to the ideas that pop into our heads, just in case their promise pans out. Equally important, we need to make a point to capture those ideas. As the Writer from Vermont, I am frequently gifted with fancy journals, which I graciously accept, even though I have never kept a journal in my life. That is not to say I do not make a point to jot down my musings on scraps of paper, or, when necessary, the palm of my hand. The other day I found a note to myself with the phrase "life's suitcase." What the heck does that even mean? I would have felt way too self-conscious committing that brain blip to a journal with an Audubon-inspired cover, but still, I wrote it down. Every expert on creativity emphasizes this practice: capture your ideas as they occur (usually during some iteration of the bed, the bath, or the bus); otherwise you will quickly forget these flashes, even the brilliant ones, guaranteed.

Here is another misperception that sabotages writers. We wait for inspiration before bothering to mosey over to our desks. The problem is, this could be a very long wait, and there goes another afternoon, or week, or sometimes a decade before we sit down to write. As Picasso famously said, "Inspiration exists, but it has to find us working."

Similarly, if we are at work and feel like we are slogging, slogging, slogging (think of the soundtrack to a forced march), we give up prematurely, assuming we cannot possibly be producing anything of merit. But feelings of frustration and even failure are part of a healthy creative process. They may not be the fun part of the process, but they are signs that you are working through challenges and stretching your creative muscles.

Given how writers tend to romanticize the notion of creativity in ways that blindside us, I wonder if we would be better served to call what we do the *not-so-creative* process. This won't feed our illusions, but it would reflect more accurately how we spend much of our time. As an instructor, I can attest to the power of the not-so-creative process because I have witnessed it countless times. When I lead writing exercises at conferences, for example, I ask participants, "Who didn't come up with anything worthwhile from the prompt?" Always, several raised hands appear, usually in the back of the room. Those are the people I call on to share what they wrote, and what I consistently hear is that what seemed like failure at the time of writing was actually flow. The moment of inspiration is not always an "Aha!" experience. More often, it is putting down one sentence after another, and trusting the current will take you around any logjams.

As an author, my own experience has helped me not just accept, but appreciate the not-so-creative process. Usually, once a book is written, it is impossible to tease out the inspired from the uninspired moments that led to its creation. Too much time has elapsed; and as with childbirth, it is best not to revisit the experience too closely if you want to have more kids. One exception stands out, however: a book I wrote several years ago. I had been excited about the topic for a long time, but only started drafting the manuscript thirteen months before it was due at the publisher. This compressed schedule meant I needed to draft a chapter a week in order to meet my deadline. The unexpected benefit of such an accelerated pace (accelerated for me, anyway) was that week after week, I witnessed a seven-day breakdown of the creative and not-so-creative process, similar to watching a seedling grow into a plant in time-lapse photography.

> Monday, excited about my great idea for a new chapter, I enthusiastically work on the lede.
> Tuesday, I have to force myself to stop reworking the lede so that I can move on, generating material, wrestling my thoughts onto the page in the order they occur. Structure will have to wait.
> Wednesday—despair! How am I ever going to turn the mess I wrote the day before into a coherent chapter? Still, given my one-chapter-a-week schedule, I must persevere, despite an overwhelming desire to nap, eat bagels, and never write again.
> Thursday, my disorganized thoughts suggest a structure, and I happily reconstitute the material. But by now, my "great idea" for the chapter is starting to feel stale, a by-product of too much familiarity.
> Friday, inspiration! Both a tighter architecture and fresh insights emerge as I focus on revision, one paragraph at a

time. My theme is discernible, albeit obscured beneath a layer of flabby language, repetition, and a brilliant description that turned out to be irrelevant, but I refuse to let it go.

> Saturday—Goodbye brilliant description; off you go to my "random musings" file. This is the day for ruthless cutting and tightening.

> Sunday—Wordsmithing. Tweaking. Polishing, not to a final draft; for that I will need some distance and feedback, but enough to reassure me I have a clean chapter that communicates what I want to say.

> Monday, excited about my great idea for a new chapter, I enthusiastically work on the lede . . .

And so a book got written, thanks in large part to the not-so-creative process. From this experience came many useful insights, including the following: Even fifteen-minute increments of writing can add up to progress. Your kids will not end up warped by watching back-to-back Disney movies when you are under deadline. And bad writing almost always gives way to good writing, not by divine intervention, but through something even more profound: the miracle of revision.

Studies have confirmed that people are motivated reasoners. We are going to believe what we want to believe, despite all evidence to the contrary. There is a name for this, confirmation bias, which means we seek out and interpret information in a way that confirms our preexisting views, while ignoring any facts that don't support our beliefs. What's more, studies show that providing corrective information only makes people—even smart, sophisticated people—double down on their misperceptions, especially when it comes to the issues they care about most—like writing.

As noted in this chapter, science has unraveled the mysteries and mythologies of the creative process. Evidence exists that writers, as a whole, are no more or less creative than the rest of humanity; the cosmos has no personal stake in our output; and an artistic muse can look a lot like yesterday's side dish. In fact, the actual act of writing bears a frighteningly close resemblance to a job, or an unpaid job depending on the circumstances. Rewards may come our way when, say, a literary journal "accepts" our work, but that sounds less like payment for services, and more like the publication is doing us a favor, similar to when the thrift store lady agrees to take my used snow pants off my hands, saying, "Someone might want them; people are pretty desperate these days."

I don't like calling writing a job any more than you like hearing it, but I do think if science and made-for-TV movies have taught us anything, it's that putting too much stock in romanticized notions almost always sets us up for failure. Of course, try telling that to the Writer from Vermont. She believes—and I hope you do too, to some degree—that writers are not like regular people. The cosmos shines down on us with a particularly bright light during our creative and even our not-so-creative moments. We imagine characters and bring them to life. We tell stories that matter to us, and we make them matter to readers. With our words, we evoke laughter, tears, transformation. Yes, inspiration exists, and it is us, made manifest in our commitment to our work, our triumphs and struggles, and the results of our hard-earned efforts. That is the view—the idyllic view—of the Writer from Vermont, as she sits on the porch swing of her rustic farmhouse, overlooking the rolling green hills.

Survival of the Optimist

Neuroscientists have determined that humans are hardwired for negativity, meaning our brains, similar to juvenile delinquents, make a point to go out and look for trouble. We are programmed to attend to, store, and recall negative information over positive information, so much so that, according to one famous finding in the realm of relationship psychology, it takes at least five positive interactions to make up for just one negative one. In science, this trait is called a negativity bias. In life, it manifests as the person no one wants to sit next to on a delayed flight from Dallas to Sydney, and given that this bias is a universal trait, that includes you and me.

Looking on the bright side, our brain's natural negativity is a good part of the reason we exist at all. In fact, early humans developed this trait as a means of survival, a way of making sure they did not overlook the woolly mammoth bearing down on them as their attention was absorbed in the scenic beauty of the grasslands. But really, nowadays, how much of a negative bias do we need to avoid being trampled by woolly mammoths? Some, to be sure, given the state of the world, but just as often these cave genetics work against us.

On any given day—I would argue even on a "bad" day—we experience many positive moments, yet these interludes barely register in our consciousness—a quick drive through our short-term memory bank. Instead, our attention dwells on the blechy stuff, real and imagined, that rarely endangers our lives but sucks the happiness from our souls. We focus on misfortunes and wrongs, like how we were not invited to the birthday party of that coworker we do not like. *Still! Everyone else in my department was invited!* We worry, even obsess, about worst-case scenarios. *What if this kale wasn't triple washed, and I die from some intestinal parasite, and my obituary in the newspaper (Just the online version? Are you frigging kidding me?) reveals that I died full of worms?* We trash talk ourselves and believe our own ridiculous slander: *I'm such a loser. I wish I were normal like everyone else. I hate my nose. I hate myself for hating my nose.*

To make matters worse, scientists claim that this persistent negative streaming leaves behind accumulating traces of neural residue that skew our brains toward an even blechier outlook. In other words, negativity literally paves the way for more negativity. My gracious, just writing about all this stuff makes me want to crawl under the covers with a copy of Schopenhauer and a glass of ice water for when I spontaneously combust.

Or it would, if neuroscience didn't also prove that we can, thank goodness, rewire our brains to override this inherent negativity bias. For this, we can credit something called neuroplasticity, the brain's ability at any age to reorganize itself by forming new neural connections. If we consciously attend to what we are thinking and feeling, we become more attuned to our body's internal sensations. If we make a point to focus on the positive, savoring the good stuff long enough for it to register, we can better store those feelings that accompany seeing a beautiful sunset, or experiencing a kindness, and in so doing we can change our brains, and thus change our behavior, and our minds.

This practice makes me think of something my friend Deb, who works for an organization dedicated to saving loons, told me. She is one of those people who radiates optimism, which cannot be easy when you work in the field of conservation funding. Still, if you tell Deb you want to do something, she will convince you that you can, help you figure out a way, and the job is as good as done. Even Deb, though, admits that her optimism is a practice as much as a personality trait. "When I drift back to the negative, I have to stop myself," she says. "It's like when you're falling asleep at your desk, and you have to consciously shake your head to wake yourself up."

In this light, maintaining a positive perspective sounds like an ongoing effort, and I suppose it is. But I would argue that it is no more effort than what it takes to get up in the morning and confront the same old same old with a miserable outlook. Think about it. What feels more worthwhile: getting through a day, or getting through a day guided by conscious choices to think and act in a way that makes you feel healthier and happier?

Of course, wouldn't you know it, even positivity comes with a downside. So although researchers have long touted the power of positive thinking to help us do everything from landing that first real job to healing more quickly after a hip replacement, more recent studies suggest that too much positive thinking can create a false sense of accomplishment that can actually be *demotivating*. Why? Because fantasizing about a happy outcome can calm us down to the degree that it saps our energy to take action toward achieving our goals. In this topsy-turvy way, positive thinking works against us. I suspect that, if anything could cheer up the curmudgeons of the world, it would be this bit of bright news from the science of motivation.

To avoid the ill effects of positive thinking, some psychologists advise people to discard all happy talk and stay focused on the hurdles that stand in the way of their desires. To this, my response is: Ugh. Wasn't dwelling exclusively on the challenges and obstacles that stood between us and our goals what stopped us in the first place, and what made us realize that we had to shift our focus to the light, because otherwise the darkness would swallow us whole? Much more to my liking are the suggestions by researchers at New York University who recommend a hybrid solution that encourages us to continue to think positively, but also to get real. This approach has been dubbed "mental contrasting," and manifests in internal monologue similar to the following:

This is doable! I can do this! I will do this! Just look at the
successful Future Me. I feel great! [Now switch gears.] Oh,
wait a second. I can do this! But first I have to stop doing this.
And start doing that. And keep my eye on the obstacles as
well as the prize. This will be challenging. This will happen.
This bouncing between realism and positivism is exhausting.

Of course, it makes sense to factor in the challenges, the workload, and the odds when setting out toward a goal. Still, just once,
I wish people would stop shushing our enthusiasm right from the
start, because, given human nature, defeatism already has the
edge. And this goes double in the creative realm.

For writers, the concepts of positive thinking and its more realistic cousin, mental contrasting, should not be ignored. Indeed, the
notion of neuroplasticity is particularly good news. I don't mean
to stereotype, but let's face it, a lot of us lug around brains with
grossly overdeveloped negativity biases, at least when it comes to
our writing lives. Even when we are actively putting words on
the page, we feel like imposters. When talking about ourselves,
we identify as "struggling artists" and "wannabes." We shame our
own drafts because of their imperfections. We denounce positive
feedback as coddling, and our need for support and community
as a weakness of will. If our efforts do not reach publication, we
feel like failures; and if we do have a book out, we feel reduced
to an Amazon ranking that will always be lower than the Amazon rankings of other authors, including some horrible, terrible,
atrocious writers who have cat detectives as their main characters. And all this internal negativity is reinforced by external messages of gloom and doom: the traditional publishing industry has
gone down the tubes; self-publishing is for hacks; no one reads
anymore; and if someone does actually purchase a book, it's only
because of something called social media, or because the writer

looks hot in his or her author photo. And last but hardly least, there are the random indignities we have to endure:

"But I thought poems had to rhyme?" (This from someone you will never show your poetry to again.)

"It's hard enough to sell a book about writing by a famous author, let alone a no-name." (This from my former agent.)

And this, the mother of indignities: "Dear Author, Thank you for your submission, I regret to inform you that your story does not fit our needs." But why not? Why doesn't your submission fit the stupid publisher's needs? And what about your need to get some recognition for all your efforts, to get some kind of sign, any sign that you are not just scribbling away the best years of your life?

These examples represent just a fraction of the types of thoughts and experiences that fill the typical writer's mind, and they explain why the default setting for so many of us could best be described as *bemoaning*. But here is the good news. None of that bad stuff really matters. Or maybe all of it matters, but certainly not all of the time.

Way back when I first started leading creative writing workshops for adults in my community, I remember having to look hard to find something nice to say about every manuscript. In those days, I was motivated to seek out the positive mostly because I didn't want to be mean, or have the writer name an ugly character after me. Actually, I still feel that way. Only now, honing in on the bright spots in a manuscript is second nature, the easiest part of my job. Though I am not a particularly sunny person in all realms of life, as a feedback provider I now find it impossible *not* to see the promising aspects of any sincere draft, no matter how faint; no matter how annoying it is to be asked to critique a single-spaced submission in nine-point type. Sometimes this ability makes me think of that kid in the movie *The Sixth Sense* who can see dead people, only I like to think that I am not as weird as him. And in fact now, according to neuroscience, I understand that my years of seeking the good in each manuscript is firsthand proof that one can indeed overwrite the brain's bias toward negativity. I know this rewiring in my head has both made me a better teacher and helped me get past the desire to set fire to any manuscript that opens with a dream. (Note to all my future students: DO NOT DO THIS. EVER.)

But, as a writer, why is this focus on the positive so important? Why is it worth our time to actively shift our attention to the bright spots in our work, as a means of overcoming our human tendency to glom onto the bad? After all, it is our bad writing that needs fixing, so isn't a focus on the good writing merely a distraction? Plus, who wants to be seen as one of those wimps who can't handle facing their failings on the page? Who wants to be associated with those touchy-feely types, people who go around saying, "I just write for myself . . ." or "It's all good," even when their verb tenses are inconsistent, or a tree randomly crushes the hood of their Kia hybrid?

I am not a neuroscientist (Bummer!), but years of experience in my own field have convinced me that the real danger to our writing lives is the very thing that once assured our existence as human beings. This negative bias—*My writing stinks! I'm not as good as the other people in my workshop! I'll never be F. Scott Fitzgerald or even Gertrude Stein!*—is ultimately what will get us in the end, if we let it. In lesser species—people not as strong or acceptably neurotic as writers—such a consistent exposure to this kind of vocational toxicity would probably fell them before breakfast. Yet we writers carry on, but at what price? And for how long?

Writers need to rewire their brains toward the positive because if we don't, sooner or later we are likely to decide that the pain and effort of capturing our stories on the page aren't worth it, even when we know writing is one of the most worthy things we can do. I have seen this happen, or almost happen, too many times. You may think I am only talking about quitter types or people who aren't really serious about their work, but in fact it is just the opposite. The real danger of a negative bias is to people like you and me, people who believe deeply in the value of writing and don't see it as a lark, yet somehow must figure out a way to see it exactly like that—a lark—at least a good part of the time.

To nurture a long and productive writing life, we must make a point to skew away from our natural negativism. We must counter the downer voices inside and outside our heads because these are the voices that discourage us from even showing up at our writing desks. These are the voices that make us second-guess every single sentence we type, even in a first draft, which happens to be the only draft where it is actually fair to say it is all good, because it is, for the time being. These are also the downer voices that make us dread revision because they direct our attention exclusively to what is not working in a manuscript.

Writing is rewriting. Duh. But this is precisely why we have to cultivate an eye toward balancing the negative with the positive. Because if we don't make a point to look beyond all the problems in our work, all we will see is a distortion of our drafts, similar to looking at a fancy hotel room through a black light. Oh my God! Through this dim perspective, all that is visible are those disgusting stains on the bedspread and carpet and walls, left by the previous guests. With that kind of shock, it's no wonder we can't even register the complimentary gift basket full of Harry and David goodies.

All this is to say, when it comes to revision, looking through a lens darkly is not only misery-making, it is counterproductive. We need to make a point to attend to the good stuff because the good stuff is the best foundation, emotionally and editorially speaking, for moving our work forward. *There, a vivid scene! There, a memorable character! There, on page thirty-seven, the real opening for the story!* This is the stuff of hope. More practically speaking, this is the stuff we can pluck from the muck and use as a foundation for a second draft. So many people approach revision by trying to fix the whole, which can feel overwhelming and result in writers wasting a lot of time reworking sections that may not even be usable or fixable. This is much less likely to happen if you focus on the promising parts, and reconstitute your work from its strengths up.

One . . . Nine . . . Seventeen . . . According to neuroscientists, it requires about thirty seconds to register an experience and begin the practice of rewiring our brains toward the positive. Yet despite the brief time commitment, the rewards are significant. With a positive bias, we feel more at peace. We develop a stronger sense of empathy that enriches humanity. We become more effective at home and work. As writers, we should be all over this good news, rocking the notion of neuroplasticity to help us see our work in a realistic, but also a positive light.

No Woolly Mammoths

Go fetch a draft right now of something you have written.
Ignore for the moment any woolly mammoths on the
page, and adjust your mindset to seek out the promising
parts. Let your attention dwell on a scene, a passage,
a word choice that evokes excitement or appreciation.
Read the strongest sections of your draft aloud. Savor
this good stuff. Nineteen . . . twenty-three . . . Remember,
thirty seconds is all it takes. Focus on the positive for now
because it is there; it is always there, so don't let your
negative bias tell you otherwise.

You Know You're Not a Writer When . . .

What is a writer? In the family of philosophical questions —Does God exist? Is pleasure possible without pain? How do you know you're not dreaming right now?—this one is on par with, say, that Kardashian brother, as insoluble as his sisters but less likely to provoke deep and prolonged examination. For those of us who care, however, the answer matters, really matters, because it can affect our sense of identity, our pride and insecurities, our motivation, and our decision to own that title in our minds, as well as when we are out in public.

"What do you do?"
"I'm a writer."
"Really. Have you written anything I would want to read?"

"What do you do?"
"I'm a writer."
"This is your lucky day! Have I got a great story for you!"

"What do you do?"
"I'm a writer."
"Me too! You should see my Christmas letters! They're hilarious!"

To weather situations like these without breathing fire, we need to feel secure in our understanding of what it means to be a writer. Without a definitive understanding of the term, we are left all too vulnerable to other people's misguided interpretations and, even more troublesome, our own peculiar notions of who is and is not "entitled" to claim this identity.

"Of course I'm not a Real Writer . . ." I hear people introduce themselves this way in workshops and at writing conferences all the time. Their reasons?

"I've only published little essays about my life, not a book or anything."

"I'm a terrible speller."

"One of my professors in graduate school told me I talk a lot better than I write." (Oh wait, this one was me, after defending a paper I had written on Cotton Mather, for which I received a C-minus.)

And yet, despite how so many of us view ourselves as imposters, here we are, working away on our very real poems and stories. So how do we explain the discrepancy? How do we manage the cognitive dissonance that comes from believing one thing that is a direct contradiction with our actions or secret ambitions?

Here is something else I hear with alarming frequency, whenever I tell people what I do for a living: "I always wanted to be a writer, but of course, now it's too late."

Too late for what? Maybe if I was chatting with these people on their deathbeds, I might see their point. Given this has never been the case, however, I feel compelled to point out that being a writer is not the same as being an Olympic gymnast. The opportunity does not go away with advancing age. We can write after we develop hips. We can write with bad knees. In fact, creative expression is often enhanced by life experience. Yes, those works your younger self might have penned are gone, but what remains are all the meaningful words worth sharing from your current perspective. So there is no such thing as coming to writing too late, only later. In fact, I believe an awareness of our diminished time on this planet offers the advantage of urgency. Recently I had lunch with a woman who spoke of a mutual friend, "I really do hope Jeffrey finishes his book before he dies."

"Jeffrey is dying?" I almost dropped my falafel wrap.

"No, but he's getting up there." I can tell you, just the thought of Jeffrey's future passing made me rethink my own tendencies to procrastinate.

Given all the confusion about what it means to be a Real Writer, I wish we had an authoritative reference, on par with the *Diagnostic and Statistical Manual of Mental Disorders*, aka the DSM-5. With such a guide, we could definitively qualify Real Writers and, equally important, disqualify those who exhibit only superficial expressions of the condition. *According to Section 8, Paragraph 49, the penning of holiday letters fails to meet the criteria of a Real Writer, and is characterized by the delusion that other people actually enjoy reading exaggerated accounts about your family's accomplishments.*

Alas, no such resource exists in the writing realm. And so, we are left to define ourselves—clearly something many of us are uniquely *un*qualified to do—or make due with the standard descriptors and characterizations. What is a writer? Probably the most common response is the following: *A writer is someone who writes.* Maybe if the question were a scientific rather than philosophical one, that answer would suffice, but philosophy is intended to go where science can't or won't, as a means of mining a deeper wisdom. Plus, this response strikes my ear as condescending, like when I look up a word in the dictionary—for example, "appropriation"—and the lexicographer deigns to offer [*uh-proh-pree-ey-shuh* n] *the act of appropriating*. Well, excuse me for asking.

Writers are also often defined, or rather maligned, through stereotypes. Think about how they are typically portrayed in the movies: the misanthrope; the drunk; the woman wrapped in an oversized sweater designed to accentuate her sexy vulnerability, staring out to sea from the deck of her multimillion-dollar beach house where she has retreated so that she can focus on finishing her next best-selling novel, while reflecting on her affair with a sexy French photographer. That woman is the opposite of real, which doesn't mean I still can't resent her.

Here is another misrepresentation of the term: *A writer is some-*

one whose work has been published. In other words, a writer is an author. I say misrepresentation here because I have a friend in Canada who teaches second grade. Each year she does a unit with her students in which they conceive and write a story, and then self-publish their little book. This is a great project, affording a wealth of teachable moments related to the creative process and collaboration. I have so much respect for educators like my friend who make writing accessible and inviting for kids. Still, when I think of the effort it took me to complete my own "little" books, and ultimately convince traditional publishers to invest in my efforts, I refuse to be lumped in with these other "authors." I am a writer. They are eight years old.

So the question remains: What is a writer? Given the evolution of publishing, we can no longer discriminate through packing labels—published, self-published, unpublished. We also cannot fully trust the literary establishment to define who is real among us. After all, not so long ago it was the publishing powers-that-be who categorically dismissed the voices of women and people of color. That is how we ended up with a literary canon that still consists mostly of "dead white guys," to quote clever English majors. Times have changed, thank goodness, but what remains is a lingering trace of systemic sexism, to name one issue. According to a recent study by VIDA, a US organization championing women in literature, almost all of the top literary magazines in the United States and Britain still reflect a disproportionate number of male reviewers of male-authored books. Given the fact that women read almost twice as many books as men, this bias is not just wrong, but bad marketing.

What is a writer? When I started working on this chapter, I was excited to put forth a definitive answer, one that would override all those other simplistic, misguided, and snobby responses. Despite my own prejudices against Canadian child authors, my goal was to democratize art, editorially speaking. My entire teaching philosophy is based on the presumption that anyone who has the guts to voluntarily show up for a writing class belongs there, and this is not as Pollyannic as it may sound. My goodness, the hopeless cases I have seen—people who seemingly lack all instincts for language; academics programmed to use twenty words when five will suffice; "novelists" who have already created tomes, but have no idea that point of view is an actual thing. And yet these people eventually proved themselves Real Writers, thanks to the transcendent power of the human spirit, in combination with a ton of narrative craft. In my clarification of the term, I wanted to make sure to convey the following: Just because you cannot write does not mean you are not a writer.

Boiled wool, fennel, people who blame their bad behavior on Mercury in retrograde. So many topics fall beyond my purview, and yet I have no trouble imposing my pontifications about them on other people. But here was a subject aligned with my professional experience and my passion, and I found myself struggling to come up with a quintessential description. What is a writer? Um. Hmm. How could any characterization possibly encompass all the manifestations of who we are, what we do, and what makes us *real*?

The best I could come up with is a sensibility, a certain awareness and responsiveness to the world. I would say if writers have anything in common, it is that we have two operating systems running at the same time: one is actively engaged in whatever situation we find ourselves in; the other is simultaneously processing whether that experience translates into potential material for our work. Say something bad happens to us. Yes, we feel sad, but, wow, that mix-up at the hospital would make a great plot point for chapter six! We take note, mentally and literally, of anybody or anything that might serve our creativity. Meaningful personal experiences are registered as possible essays. We log the idiosyncrasies of family members, friends, and strangers to inform our characters. We eavesdrop on conversations because we are nosy, and with an ear toward converting speech to dialogue.

In a way, this dual processing means that writers are not just people who write, but people who are always writing, even when we are nowhere near a computer or can't find a pen in our purses. (You would think this would not keep happening.)

The fact that we are constantly on the lookout for material may be partly why writers have a reputation as being discomfiting to be around at times. As Joan Didion wrote, "Writers are always selling someone out." As someone who favors writing in the personal essay genre, I like to think I am not quite that exploitative. I also take comfort in the fact that every discipline has its distinct peculiarities. I suspect dermatologists, for example, also see people through two lenses, first as people, but also as their skin conditions. In this light, I would argue that writers are at least better company than dermatologists, because I, for one, would rather be seen as inspiration for a character than as a suspicious mole.

Still, I continued to struggle with a definitive answer to the question of what constitutes a writer, until one day I had an epiphany. It happened toward the end of a workshop. The group members were offering feedback to a woman I will rename Winnie, because I don't like that name, and I did not care for how she was always sketching in her notebook during class, probably creating caricatures of the rest of us as we discussed the stories on the table. Winnie's submission elicited the usual mix of positive and critical comments—some spot on, some from left field, but all of them, to my ear, well intentioned. Here is a condensed transcript:

FEEDBACK PROVIDER: "I don't think you need to introduce
    all your characters on page one . . ."
WINNIE: "But they're all important to the story . . ."

FP: "I had a hard time following the scene on page seven . . ."

w: "But that part really happened to me. I didn't even make
it up."

FP: "The story's sudden switch in point of view was
confusing . . ."

w: "There's no other way to show what the cab driver is
thinking . . ."

A lot of writers get defensive when people criticize their work.
Sometimes my own first impulse in the face of negative feedback
is to get mad at the reader because, clearly, the person is clueless,
even if right. But the reality is that feedback—positive and negative—is a godsend that can energize our creativity, save us time,
and help us hone our editorial instincts. In fact, I would argue
that feedback is often the difference between writing and not
writing, and between writing and writing well. Most of my workshop participants come to quickly appreciate reader responses to
their works-in-progress. Winnie, on the other hand, only grew
more defensive as the workshop continued, which, in turn, made
me feel more defensive as the instructor.

"How come you always encourage everybody else," she confronted me toward the end of her story discussion, "but you never
say anything positive to me?"

Oh, puh-leeze! I thought. Or at least I hope I didn't say it aloud.
Stop being such a big baby. I have enough EQ to understand how
emotion can distort our ability to hear. When it comes to criticism, some writers can choke on a crumb, and it is my job, and
your job as a feedback provider, to weigh all the brilliant, constructive things we have to say against what the writer can actually process at any given moment before having a meltdown.
Normally, I am good at working with writers with tender egos (it
takes one to know one), but not in this case, not when the person
is a sketcher. In my mind's eye, I could just imagine Winnie's cari-
cature of me—a blowsy blonde with devil horns and fangs.

After Winnie's accusation, the others compensated for my apparently noxious behavior with a flurry of encouraging words. *The people in this group are so nice*, I thought, which is something I often think during workshops. One of the best parts of my job is bearing witness to the loveliness of a supportive writing community. But then I looked at Winnie, and thought something I hardly ever think: *You will never be a writer.*

That's when it struck me that the only way to answer the question that had been vexing me since I began writing this chapter was through a negative definition. What is a writer? Too many variables, too many manifestations, too many unpredictabilities disallow a conclusive response. Yet, what can be pinpointed is what a writer is *not*. Similar to a diagnosis of exclusion in medicine—that is identifying something by it not being other things—it occurred to me that this is also the most reliable way to determine who is a Real Writer, and whether we qualify.

With this in mind, I came up with a list of characterizations—a short list, as it turns out—that negatively defines a writer. If you find that you are none of these things, then you can safely assume that you are real. It is that simple. It is that important. You may be unpublished, you may struggle to acquire craft, and others may discount your voice, your genre, your aspirations, but if you assume you are a writer, if you claim that title in your head and heart, good things will happen. You will take yourself and your work more seriously. Without the distraction of an identity crisis, you will commit more fully to doing what Real Writers do, which is believe you have something to say, and then figure out a way to communicate it on the page.

You Know You're Not a Writer When ...

You can't handle constructive criticism. Writers want their work to have power, to communicate, to engage and entertain, to mean something to people other than themselves. They don't blame the reader if they fail. If you can't get past your insecurity or ego to hear where your writing needs improvement, invest in a diary and keep your thoughts to yourself.

You won't revise. Writing is rewriting. It is not simply transcribing to the page the stories you make up in your head. It is not settling for good enough, just because you prefer the rush of a new story idea, or have grown tired of revisiting the same piece. If you are not open to revising, or putting in the time to polish your work, you are only half a writer, and not necessarily the better half.

You can't separate writing from ranting. I knew a talented wordsmith who could have been a writer, if it wasn't for her ex-husband. In the personal essays she worked on during the time I knew her, she could not *not* slam her "wasband," as she called him. She told her readers repeatedly what an asshole he was, which was one of her kinder descriptions of him. Essayists have agendas—that is a good part of why we write, to share our truths. But we will never get readers to see what we want them to see, or come around to our way of thinking, if we force our judgments on them. "Show, don't yell," I said to the woman with the wasband. Sometimes even bad humor can dispel enough anger to make room for craft. "But he is such an asshole!" she persisted, which may very well be the case, I thought, but only a writer can make me believe it.

You don't want to be a writer. Once upon a time I finished a book, and decided I was done. So I stopped all that dual processing in my head and did other meaningful things, like decorate the house with giant, fake cobwebs for Halloween. This was something I had done every year since my daughters were little, but now I took great pleasure in the arrangement of the web, and the placement of each dangling plastic spider, even though by this time my girls were teenagers and failed to share my enthusiasm. My cobweb phase lasted about two years, during which time I loved not writing . . . until I didn't. What this experience taught me is that there will always be days, weeks, months, even years in your life when you are not writing, but those times only feel great when you are not a writer.

You let others discourage you. Good riddance, I thought as Winnie packed up at the end of class. Her story discussion had ended on a civilized note, but when she walked by me to leave, I could see in her face that she was still upset. *You will never be a writer.* It actually gave me a pang to think this about her; to think this about anyone who clearly cares about writing. The following week, as anticipated, Winnie did not show up for class. She did, though, to my surprise, return for the remaining sessions, and the work she put forth revealed that she had listened to the group's feedback and was willing to revise. She also dropped a good bit of her defensiveness, though her drawings may tell another story. Regardless, Winnie and all those sketchy types like her can teach us an important lesson: If a writing instructor, even one so intimidating as to sport devil horns and fangs, thinks that you will never be a writer, that does not necessarily make it true. Unless, of course, you decide to believe it.

In Good Company

I was sitting on a bench in the Mall of New Hampshire, eating pretzel nuggets, when a couple holding hands drew my attention. One cannot help what goes through one's head, and when I saw them, I thought of those calendars that depict unusual animal friends. She, tiny, with a sprout of gray, frizzled hair, would be an aye-aye; he a blobfish with his large form and aspic pallor. In a world where so many people are adrift, here were two individuals who had managed to connect against the odds. And across species. The afterthought popped into my head, but not in a mean way.

I can be stonehearted when it comes to certain displays of sentiment: singing telegrams at the office; marriage proposals on the fifty-yard line; strewn rose petals that somebody is going to have to clean up. Suddenly, however, I found myself wishing that I was holding a hand instead of a pretzel nugget. One of my daughters was in a store nearby shopping for a prom dress, but even if I tracked her down, she had put the kibosh on holding my hand around the time she started writing in cursive. I only prayed that she would find it in her heart to acquiesce on my deathbed. But what to do in the meantime? Here I was in a busy mall, surrounded by shoppers and retailers with ridiculously generous sizing, and yet I felt alone, even lonely.

This is when the idea struck me. A hand-holding business! A service that provides anyone with a hand to hold whenever they feel alone. Outside of leasing sleepy kittens, what faster way to help people feel better instantly? The business could borrow from the model of traditional dating websites, in that members joined online to find or be matched with others seeking this kind of platonic connection. Or it could be run like a social service, where hand-holders paid home visits to get clients through a difficult situation or transition. One division could include a hand-holder temp service, ideal for people on the job, interested in a short-term solution to their need for connection.

"My three-o'clock just canceled. Can you send someone over to hold my hand ASAP?"

"No problem!"

Individuals, corporations, prisons, schools, nursing homes: my hand-holding business could serve them all as part of a roster of wellness initiatives, similar to other out-of-the-box options like laughter yoga and treadmill desks. Studies have confirmed that nonsexual touch has a profound impact on our emotional and physical well-being. Related to this, social psychologists have shown that a sense of belonging is foundational to success, and that social isolation is a serious health risk, linked to impaired immune function and increased inflammation that can lead to heart disease and other unpleasant conditions. Research suggests the increased mortality risk among lonely people is comparable to that from smoking, and twice as dangerous as obesity. Imagine if these risks could be reduced with a simple invitation, "Come, take my hand."

I have run my business idea by several friends who, surprisingly, failed to share my enthusiasm.

"What if I don't like the person?"

"What if it makes me feel self-conscious to be touching someone I've just met?"

"What if they have sweaty palms?"

What if . . . What if . . . What if . . . And I thought these people were my friends. Of course, this is what good ideas are up against: the human tendency to see problems instead of solutions. This is yet another way we inadvertently thwart our own happiness, allowing our fear of social discomfort to trump the need for connection. *This Friday*, we tell ourselves, *I am going to that contra dance at town hall!* We don't know exactly what contra dancing is, but we do know that people say it is fun, and we need to get out more. But then this Friday, like so many other Fridays, rolls around and suddenly we are overtaken by exhaustion at 7 p.m., just when the time comes to leave the house. So we get in our comfies and binge watch all five seasons of a canceled show we didn't even care about the first time it aired, and then we wake up grumpy the next morning and make another promise to ourselves. *Next Friday, I will go to the contra dance in town hall . . . though weren't the contras part of some kind of political scandal in the eighties?*

That, my friend, is how easy it is to find reasons to avoid connection, even when a folk dance that just happens to share a name with a US-backed terrorist rebel group in Nicaragua may be exactly the cure for what ails you.

Writers are loners. So goes the myth that feeds into one of our most counterproductive instincts, which is to hole away and hide our work-in-progress (or lack of progress) when we are feeling alone or going off the deep end. For most of us, this fear-induced mentality (Don't put yourself out there! Don't let others see your struggle!) cuts us off from the very thing that could benefit us most—a writing community. The resistance to my hand-holding idea was mild compared to what I have heard after suggesting to frustrated writers—people clearly in need of inspiration and a reality check—that they join a writing group. For example:

"But what if I don't feel ready to share my work?"

"What if everybody else is better than me?"

"What if I don't like the other people, and then I'm stuck listening to a bunch of losers tell me what's wrong with my writing?"

What if . . . What if . . . What if . . . Take note of how these unhappy writers feed their own unhappiness by allowing potential problems they have manufactured in their minds deny them a possible solution to the very real issues they are facing in the here and now. Even when we recognize the toll isolation is taking on us, we often feel too ashamed by our need for connection or validation to take action. To admit this would be the equivalent of wearing a big *L* on our foreheads. Real writers work alone! Real writers don't need someone to hold their hand and tell them they are worthy. Time passes and these misperceptions become entrenched. Rather than reaching out, we become more practiced at social evasion, going out of our way to avoid interactions with people we do not know or trust. The idea of talking to a stranger, especially about our writing, seems inconceivable. Evolutionary psychologists attribute this counterproductive behavior to a leftover survival instinct. *Stay on the periphery! Avoid any and all risks!* These are the misguided thought bubbles of the lonely mind.

I once read that the average determined smoker makes 4.1 attempts to quit smoking before finally succeeding. By my calculation, this is also the same number of times the average determined writer decides to join a writing workshop, before actually showing up at one. If we have to resort to labels, then I would say those people are the Real Writers, the ones who have the gumption to set aside their fears, or anxieties, or snobbishness, or misguided notions, and get the support they need to accomplish their goals. I think anyone who engages in continuing education has a lot on the ball, but in my biased opinion, people who enroll in writing classes should get bonus points for extra initiative, even courage, because so much more is required of them than listening and learning.

"You mean I would actually have to write something?" People sometimes ask me this when inquiring about my workshops. Their voices reveal their trepidation.

I do everything short of handing out Valiums to reassure anxious newcomers that no harm will come to them by joining a

group. "Of course you will fit in! Everybody fits in!" My exuber-
ance is often enough to inch people through the door of my little
writer's center, which is a good start. But the fear of writing really
has only one proven alleviant: you have to write your way through
it. I know of some MFA classes that are more lecture based, but I
think the littlest amount of disquisition goes a long way. Character development! Plot devices! Objective co-relatives! It can all
sound like theoretical mush, unless discussed within the context
of a student's own work.

There is no way around this. To reap the most value from writing classes and groups requires that we put pen to page, and offer
up our work to others for feedback. How nerve-wracking is that,
to sit among strangers and be expected to expose on paper our
most meaningful memories, our beliefs and feelings, our idea
for a mythopoeic novel set in the fictional universe of Xialandia.
What if everybody thinks you are a terrible person just because
you shared in writing that you hate yoga? What if they tell you
the concept of your novel is ridiculous, and you are already 593
pages into it? Even worse, what if they think you are simply a terrible writer? Any feedback interaction runs the risk of feelings
being hurt; and even benign comments can be taken to heart in
the wrong way. I once presented an essay for feedback to a friend,
and his only response via email was to point out the misuse of
the past perfect progressive tense in a particular sentence. (I will
have been stewing about this friend's comment for nearly eight
years now.)

So I get it. I really do. I have been writing forever, and I can still
be a chicken when it comes to inviting outsiders into the sanc-
tum sanctorum of my creative mind. Particularly the first time
I expose a new piece for feedback, I imagine the response being
some kind of medical event. *Oh my God, he thinks the idea is so stupid he seized.* Given my random bouts of insecurity, it comes as
no surprise to me that I would be the one to conjure up the idea

for a hand-holding service. Every time I sit down to reread one of my early drafts, or await reviews of a newly released book, I wish someone was right there beside me, gently squeezing my typing fingers and telling me that everything is going to be okay.

I hate to admit this, given that writers already have more than their share of imaginary problems, but experience has taught me that some of the fears that feed our instincts to hole up with our drafts are well founded. There are dangers, real dangers out there in even the most innocent-looking writing communities. They take the form of people, including peers and authority figures, including friends and frenemies, who give us lunatic advice, say mean things, and can break our spirit all too easily, if we let them. Note the clause at the end of that sentence, *if we let them*. I once had a professor so toxic that his influence brought me *this close* to writing myself off. For that, I should thank him for allowing me to prove that I am not the big baby I sometimes think I am. A few years later, when I started teaching, my guiding philosophy was to do exactly the opposite of what he did. Oh, how I wish I could name names! (Okay, his first name starts with A.) I am sad to say that this anti-educator continues to poison the minds of creative writing students even to this day, thanks to the dark side of tenure.

And then there are the other potential dangers out there, not just in classrooms but in cyberspace and beyond. I have had only limited experience with online writing communities, but I have heard stories about comments shared in certain chat rooms that make the haters on TMZ seem charitable by comparison. Warnings should also accompany participation in literary conferences and networking events. I once attended a prestigious conference that hosted a panel consisting of a celebrity author, two top agents, and a hungry-looking young editor from a big publishing house in New York City. Their expert consensus was that all the aspiring authors in the audience should give up on trying to sell their manuscripts. "I feel sorry for writers," said one of the agents, while the other panelists nodded in doleful unison.

At another conference, a distinguished poet and head of a creative writing program at a Midwestern university sat across from me at dinner. I told him I was interested in taking a particular online poetry-writing course that came highly recommended. "Don't waste your time with classes. Poetry should be learned by reading." And this from a poetry instructor. Later in the conversation, it came up that I was working on a book about the creative process, to help writers understand that there is more than one right way to write. "Writers already have too many rules," he said, waving his hand in dismissal. But hadn't I just made that very same point? How could he be criticizing my concept and underscoring it at the same time? "Plus," he added, "I don't know what that is, *the creative process*." Was he kidding? It's not like I had invented a completely new term. *Yes, I'm working on a book about oshgiblah. What do you think?*

I have found this is a trademark among a subset of academics— this proclivity to be willfully oppositional, to argue against everything, just for the sake of argument. Particularly annoying is when an instructor takes the stance that creative writing cannot be taught, a comment I hear with alarming frequency. But then, pray tell, how do those who make this claim justify their paychecks?

Also not to be overlooked are the risks associated with simply socializing with other writers. I am still wary after attending a particular "Writer's Night Out" in my region where I had to endure a one-sided conversation about gender politics, a subject that normally interests me, but how many times can one hear the word "hegemonic" and not want to scream? Never have I been more aware of the design flaws of the long, rectangular table, where you are confined to the company of the pontificator on your left, while the people seated at the far end of the table seem to be having the time of their lives. I also have attended more than a few casual gatherings among writers, including parties of my own making, where sometime in the evening fellowship gave way to feuding, most recently over that plastic thingie in the game Catch Phrase.

Would I like those particular hours of my life back? You bet I would. Still, those few, unfortunate experiences are nothing compared to the immeasurable value I have gained from being in the company of other writers across all sorts of settings. I once spent two weeks at a residency for artists and writers in a remote Vermont town in the dead of winter. We were housed in a building with thin walls, so I could hear every word of the phone conversation between my neighbor and her mother. I learned more than I wanted to about her sister's breakup with her boyfriend (on Valentine's Day!) and the upcoming forecast for that week, which involved ice a quarter inch thick. Then the mother asked how the residency was going, and my neighbor replied, "Really good. I think being around other writers legitimizes the process, like we're all in it together." *It does legitimize the process!* I agreed from the other side of the wall. *Why, it's almost like we're all in it together in the same room.*

There is a photographer in New York who enlists strangers walking down the street to pose together as if they are family. He arranges them in ways suggestive of warm, loving relationships— arms draped around each other's shoulders, bodies leaning in for support. *Uh, okay?* At first, a lot of the participants do not see the point. Their body language reveals their initial awkwardness. But then something happens; they quickly begin to relax into their roles. The shared experience engenders feelings of safety and intimacy. You can see it in the photographs. The diverse couples and small groups actually have the look of loving family members. The people in the photos say they even felt like family when creating the portraits together. This unexpected gift, this connection through proximity and a collective purpose, is the same thing that can happen when you open yourself up to a writing community.

For the record, I know that my hand-holding business will never fly, especially in America, reputed to be one of the most touch-phobic countries in the world. Regardless, I still think it is a good idea. I still believe we can address at least some of the ills of the world, and in our own minds, by starting with a simple invitation.

Come, take my hand. Even if it feels contrived. Even if you are already in your comfies. Even if you have sweaty palms. I cannot explain the mysteries of the human spirit, but I do know that something transformative happens when we interact with others striving for similar goals. As writers, to be part of a creative community is to sheathe ourselves in white light. That white light stays with us, sometimes long after we return to the solitude that our work demands. It illuminates the vast difference between loneliness and being alone, and within that clarified space this is what often happens: We write more. We write better. And we are happier. Or maybe it's the other way around.

Five Reasons to Consider a Workshop

Pop! Think of a workshop as a "social-belonging intervention," a way to gang up on a writer in a nice way. In a group, you can feel reassured that even if you have lost perspective and hope, your fellow participants, or at least some of them, will be there to help you snap out of it. "Don't give up now! Write! Rewrite! You'll feel better soon!" In return for this reality check, you can then offer that same service to the other group members, when they are the ones in need of support. In short, being part of a workshop or any type of writing exchange pops the "pluralistic ignorance bubble," in which everyone thinks she is the only one having trouble. Much comfort (and confidence) can be derived from the following truth: Writing is hard for everyone.

Bigmindedness. In any new writing group, you are going to find yourself in the company of amazing talents, as well as some person you would not have chosen to hang out with in a million years. In regard to the latter, a workshop affords you the perfect opportunity to overcome any small-mindedness on your part, which you cannot tell me is not one of your goals. Psychologists have consistently found that when unlikely people gather in a safe environment around a valuable experience, their negative feelings toward each other tend to dissipate, and are replaced by more complex, empathetic emotions. The experts call this intergroup contact theory. I call it a typical writing workshop. Imagine, literary and genre novelists sitting side by side, coming to recognize their shared humanity, while appreciating each other's unique attributes. And, of course, their bond is made even stronger through their mutual suspicion of those weirdoes who write flash fiction.

Momentum. A lot of participants take my workshops several times in a row to keep up their writing momentum. Then they stop, maybe because they need a break, or maybe because they begin to question the authority of an instructor who carries around a folder with a picture of two French bulldog puppies on the cover. (Aren't French bulldogs adorable?!)

I cannot emphasize enough how workshops are a great resource when you need instruction, motivation, and accountability. But I also know that even good writing groups can become a distraction. When that time comes, it makes perfect sense to retreat and write on your own. Often, I will encounter former participants around town whose names I may have forgotten, but rarely their stories.

"How's your book coming?" I might ask, depending on the person. Posing this question can be the verbal equivalent of sticking your finger into the cage of a conure; you just never know how it will fly. Still, there are times when it seems like a reasonable query. "As I recall, you were making great progress!"

"I haven't written a word for months."

Well, how can I not be a little satisfied to hear this news?

Clearly, my workshop services are needed. Or maybe the real takeaway from this cautionary tale is to ask yourself three simple questions: (1) What have you done in the past that has fed your writing momentum? (2) Why don't you just do that again? And, (3) Seriously, aren't French bulldog puppies adorable?!

5.3 Years. There are people—okay, mostly men (excuse me if this sounds sexist)—who seem to lack the ability to join things, and by things I mean writing groups and choral societies. But why? Men like to write. Men like to sing. Men also crave connection, as I was reminded yet again at a recent conference that drew writers from all over the country.

"I wish I had something like this where I live," said a young man to me over breakfast. He told me he was an English lit teacher at a community college, and was at the conference to work on his poetry with like-minded writers.

"Why don't you start a poetry writing group?" I asked. "Or take a workshop where you live and then pick some people you like from it to exchange drafts."

"I don't do that!" He rejected the idea before I had barely finished my sentence, as if I had suggested swapping wives instead of poems. Or maybe that idea would have been met with more careful consideration.

Sometimes I look at the disproportionate ratio of women to men in my classes (on average six to two), and I wonder why. Is there a gene linked to the Y chromosome that prohibits joining? Maybe this helps to explain the mystery of the gender gap in life expectancy, and why women live on average 5.3 years longer. Think about this the next time you dismiss outright the notion of a writing workshop (or choral society). Would it kill you to join, or (gasp) to initiate a group? Or would it possibly give you a longer, happier life?

More Is More. When I first started teaching, there was a great guy in one of my workshops who wanted me to meet his wife because he thought we would hit it off. Yes! I agreed, because, at that point in my life, my social circle consisted mostly of my neighbor's cat.

"You should meet Joni," he went home and told her.

"I don't need another friend," she replied. Her life was full. She had recently finished an MBA program, and was starting a business. *Well then*, I thought, feeling rejected. *Be that way.* But then, a few months later, we met by chance, and her husband was right —we did hit it off and have been great friends for almost two decades. Way back when, this was the woman who was watching my six-month-old daughter when she rolled over for the first time and fell off the bed. The baby was fine. My friend was a wreck. In fact, what she needed most in that moment was another friend, like me, to reassure her that these things happen, and to not say what I was really thinking, which was this: *I told you so. We all need more friends, even when we think we don't.*

What a Week!

Like a lot of schools, the one in my town welcomes people as they drive onto the campus with a big, electronic message board announcing the latest student birthdays, upcoming dates for standardized testing (always more standardized testing), and other important events. One Monday, the message board shared this happening: "Don't forget! It's Middle School Kindness Week!"

Oh dear.

You know the situation is dire once someone decides to designate a special time slot to acknowledge it. The pattern has long been established of devoting a day, a week, even an entire month to certain causes and people, a Who's Who of the historically underappreciated or seriously wronged: Secretary's Day, Mother's Day, Older Americans Month . . .

At the middle school, Kindness Week could have been dubbed Dweeb Week, because likely the event was a thinly disguised effort to raise awareness of the plight of those kids who have suffered the most from adolescent insensitivity.

"Wanna help support my trip to the Anime Convention by buying a Death Note cupcake?" asks the awkward middle schooler, her changing body caught at the crossroads of baby fat and busty.

"Uh, sure, I guess so," says the star of the eighth grade class, because he is actually a sweet boy underneath all that cool, and a Death Note cupcake is still a cupcake.

If ever there was a time for the dweebs of the world to clean up on fundraising, this would be the week.

At first I thought Kindness Week was a great idea; I am all for encouraging or coercing people into being good to one another. But then as Monday gave way to Tuesday and then the next thing I

knew it was Friday, I no longer liked the notion that a call for kindness should come with an end date. What did that open the door
to for the rest of the school calendar? Mean Girls Week? Towel-
Snapping Week? And what was wrong with middle schoolers anyway? To see them at drop-off looking so innocent and adorable,
weighted down with their ridiculously heavy backpacks and in-
strument cases and sports paraphernalia, only to be reminded that
kindness is something that needs to be curricularized, not unlike
pre-algebra or frog dissection. If only kindness came naturally; if
only it were as intrinsic for tweens as the impulse to look at their
reflections in every available mirror or glass surface they pass.

Long after Kindness Week had come and gone, I continued
to dwell on the need for this type of campaign, and what it said
about humanity, well beyond the hormone-filled hallways of middle school. As is often the case when thinking crosses the line into
overthinking, I began to find fault with this well-intentioned effort, starting with its core concept—*kindness*.

According to Scripture, kindness is an attribute of God, made
manifest in grace, even toward those creatures who are wicked
or ungrateful. Here on earth, our job is to emulate that divine behavior in the form of human kindness. Believer, nonbeliever, unless you are a sociopath, who can't get behind the idea of a week
that encourages everyone to behave more like divinity? But that
was part of my nit with Kindness Week. It left a tincture of sanc-
timony in my mouth, probably because someone sometime in my
unresolved past had done something kind for me when I was feeling low, and then gotten all smug about it. Still, you *bestow* a kindness, which could run the risk of the giver being seen as a bit
holier than thou, and the recipient as having some sort of special
need or affliction. Say you end up in the hospital with appendici-
tis, so now—as opposed to last winter when you wanted to go to
Vegas to gamble—your older brother and his wife (who selfishly
chose not to have kids, or even a dog, so that they could do what-

ever they want whenever they want) agree to take your brood for the weekend. So yes, they did you a kindness, but first you had to suffer a near miss of peritonitis.

Given that kindness often manifests when one party has the advantage over the other, it strikes me more as a form of charity —the pity sex of thoughtful behaviors. Is this the type of behavior we want our middle schoolers to dwell on for an entire week? I am not so sure. And while kindness sets the bar high in terms of consciousness raising, when it comes to making good behavior a cause, my own preference would be to bring the bar back down to earth. Why not devote a week to a more common, egalitarian type of goodness? Why not start a campaign to promote a manner of conduct available to everybody, the haves and the have-nots, the gamblers and their relatives, the stars of the eighth grade class and the dweebs?

I am talking, surprise, surprise, about *niceness*. Basic human niceness, a cause less lofty than kindness, but no less worthy; a cause that does not receive a fraction of the attention or respect that kindness receives, and yet! If people were simply nice to one another and to themselves, we could make every, single day more pleasant. We could give real meaning to the comment, "Have a nice day." Indeed, we could change our individual and collective existence on this earth for the better, and no one would have to bestow anything on anybody.

There is no denying that niceness often gets a bad rap in the real world, but it is also underappreciated and viewed with suspicion in the writing world, as the following story exemplifies. Last summer I went to the funeral of an acquaintance I will call Misty. After the service, attendees were invited to share stories about the deceased as a way of celebrating her life. A man with a long gray ponytail stood up and shared that he and Misty had been in a playwriting group together.

"I remember running into Misty at the checkout at the food co-op," he said. "Out of the blue she started criticizing a script I'd shown her awhile back. 'That line didn't work . . . That part was nonsense . . . I didn't like your ending . . .' That was Misty." The aging hippie looked around the room at her friends and family, all smiling in fond remembrance. "She really let you have it when she didn't like your work, whereas everyone else was just nice."

Just nice. This is a common pairing of words, as in only or merely nice; as in not-to-be-trusted nice. It's as if somewhere along the way, the word "nice" hired a grossly inept public relations person who allowed its connotation to be railroaded far from its original meaning of pleasant and agreeable. When I was working on this chapter, I did an informal survey among members of my own writing community, asking them for their connotation of the word.

"Ugh. You can't trust people who are nice."

"It sounds fake, like they're just being polite."

"If someone says to me, 'That's a nice dress,' I think, *Bitch.*"

There were those telling comments, and then there was this story that, oddly enough, involved a semantic debate identical to the one that prompted this chapter. "Last Sunday, the minister at my church did a sermon about the difference between being kind and being nice," another workshop participant shared, "and what he said was that the difference between kindness and niceness is honesty."

"Which one lacks honesty?" I asked.

"Niceness!" The other workshop participants responded in chorus, as if the answer was obvious.

That is how bad things have become for niceness, when even from the pulpit we are told that pleasantness equates to lying. Conversely, kindness must have the best public relations rep in the universe, judging by its popularity on bumper stickers and beyond. Random Acts of Kindness has become a mantra, a week, a foundation, a worldwide movement. This is all to the good, but it also speaks to my point. Kindness is an act. It is something you do that serves another person and humanity, and it makes you feel good in the process. Niceness is a state of being. It is how you are, or should be, as a person and citizen of the world. Niceness, real niceness, not the besmirched version of the concept, should be the agar of engagement, the culture medium of how we conduct our everyday lives, and the context in which we pursue our writing lives.

A disclosure. Part of the reason I am motivated to restore the good name of niceness is that I have been personally affected by this issue. In my own work as a writing instructor and editor, I have been called "nice" by a good many students and clients, sometimes to my face. Even when people have not called me this directly, my professional reputation was bound to get back to me, given that I live and work in a small town, and the MFA programs where I teach insist that their students write faculty evaluations.

I once saw a graphic t-shirt that read, "You call me a freak like that's a bad thing." That is how I feel when writers say I am nice. I have long sensed this comment was, at best, a backhanded compliment, but now, thanks to an understanding of how the writing world views this state of being, I can better translate the actual meaning behind these evaluations:

"You are nice because you think all writing is good, even when it sucks." (Read: *Not like Misty, who really lets people have it!*)

"You are nice because you don't like confrontation." (Read: *Liar!*)

"You are nice because you hate my writing." (Read: *Bitch!*)

Actually, one of those assessments is true. I do not like confrontation. In fact, I am someone who, at the first sign of tension, wrings her hands and tries to defuse the situation, if only in my head. *Goodness gracious, people. It's not like we don't have enough real problems in the world. Let's just all say we're sorry and move on. Death Note cupcake, anyone? Anyone?*

Regardless of my dislike of confrontation, the idea that my niceness equates to lying about the value of a manuscript, or a lack of discernment on my part when it comes to quality work, makes no sense. It also makes me mad. One look at the critiques I provide on students' manuscripts makes it clear that my message as an instructor is that writing is rewriting, and good is never good enough. I simply offer my critiques nicely, meaning I criticize specific aspects of the writing, but not the writer. I focus on the positive, as a way to highlight narrative techniques in the work worth replicating. I also work under the assumption that the student is a capable human being; and, last but hardly least, I am purposely not mean or insulting because, contrary to some popular opinions, this does nothing to serve the educational interaction, in fact quite the opposite.

And herein lie the dangers when writers perceive niceness as a form of lying or ineptitude. We fail to hear or trust the good things that are being said about our work, even though we absolutely, to a person, need to hear those good things to keep writing.

"My friends tell me I'm a good writer, but they're my friends so their opinions don't count." Writers say things like this all the time. (Also typically discounted are the opinions of mothers and spouses.) But the opinions of people who say nice things about your work do count. These nice comments may not be a substitute for more detailed feedback or constructive criticism, but they provide an important perspective, as well as a softer landing for the harsher words that are likely to follow. For this reason alone, we should take all nice comments about our work to heart, and keep them there.

On a related note, it's important to cultivate niceness in our writing groups and feedback partnerships; otherwise we cheat ourselves of not only a more pleasant working environment, but a more productive one. Niceness is like an energy-saving light bulb. It fills the room with agreeable light, enabling us to do our work more efficiently without wasting our already limited emotional resources. Bathed in this glow, we are now more capable of thoughtful discourse, lowering our defenses, and allowing for consideration of constructive suggestions.

Yet another reason to campaign for niceness is that, if we fail to establish this as standard behavior within the writing community at large, we leave ourselves vulnerable to nefarious influences. I am talking about nastiness, and its little toadie, snark. These two malignancies already have insinuated their ugly charms into our culture. Consider the following two articles, typical of a genre of writing on writing. One piece ran in the *New York Times* book section, and was a diatribe about the problem with memoirs. The writer bemoaned the "lost art of shutting up," and the days when you had to "earn the right" to draft memoir by accomplishing something noteworthy. "Unremarkable lives went unremarked upon, the way God intended." The author's point? As far as I can tell, there wasn't one, other than to discount people's lives and discourage them from writing.

The other piece exhibited an equal amount of vitriol. This article first appeared in *The Stranger*, Seattle's alternative weekly newspaper. The author, once an instructor in an MFA program, trashed his old job and former students, and ranted about the narcissism of memoirists. (It has occurred to me that the sport of mocking memoirists is the equivalent of shooting fish in a barrel.) In one of the more notable passages in the article, the author shared, "Just because you were abused as a child does not make your inability to stick with the same verb tense for more than two sentences any more bearable. In fact, having to slog through 500 pages of your error-riddled student memoir makes me wish you had suffered more."

This is what niceness is up against: these nasty voices that say little of value, but are assigned an authority too often presumed when people are really good at clever, noxious commentary.

These are the voices that will drown our ambitions, our sanity, and our humanity, if we throw niceness under the bus. These are the voices that pave the way for more and more demagogues, until eventually we end up with a writing atmosphere so toxic that even allegedly "nice" people like me resort to name-calling and throwing stupid articles by stupid people up against the wall. *Unremarkable lives, my ass!*

And another thing! These articles could have used their column inches for good, rather than evil. If we are experiencing an epidemic of poorly written memoirs, then why not offer a thoughtful analysis of the problem? Why not discuss the challenges inherent in the genre, like the negotiation between truth and facts? Why not explain the sweet spot of memoir, that intersection of the personal and universal, the ordinary and the historical? Why not address specific failings of MFA programs, rather than condemn those students who pay good money to attend them? Even better, why not celebrate the reality that the rise in memoir has less to do with narcissism, and everything to do with the growing recognition that every life—not just the lives of the powerful or notorious—is noteworthy? Every life, if rendered artistically on the pages, has the capacity to reveal the life of the times. Every person is an agent of history. Indeed, there are about forty gazillion worthwhile insights those authors could have volunteered on the subject of memoirs, not one of them wishing a victim of child abuse more suffering.

If niceness were the norm in our culture, then screeds, vitriol, and every other form of hurtful hissy fit would be dismissed as unsuitable for publication. "Much ado about nothing," the editor of the *New York Times* book section would conclude after reading the submission on the problem with memoirs. And the rant sent along to the Seattle paper by the former MFA teacher? "Well, to the poor author's credit," the editor would say, shaking his head in befuddlement at the lack of maturity and discipline of some writers, "he certainly knows how to put the mean in meaningless."

I know promoting niceness as a way of being in the writing world, let alone the world at large, will be an uphill battle. I know it may do my reputation as an instructor even further damage, not just exacerbating a mistrust of my authority, but inviting comparisons to those other nice people, the ones who go around saying questionable things like, "How about a group hug?" and "If you can't say anything nice, then don't say anything at all." These are risks I am willing to take.

For one designated week, the middle school in my town reminded students and everyone who drove by its message board to act with kindness. Despite all my overthinking, I recognize that this was a lovely effort. But let's not give all our attention to random acts of charitable behavior, and think that our work is done. This leaves too many holes in the calendar year for making life miserable for each other and for ourselves. The time has come to elevate niceness to the rank of kindness.

"It's Be Nice to Everybody Week!" If I ran the middle school in my community, or better yet the world, this would be the announcement on my message board, which would actually look more like a giant marquee surrounded by flashing pink lights. And I would showcase that message fifty-two weeks a year, along with birthday greetings to everyone on the planet. This would be my way of making the world a more pleasant and agreeable place. This would be my form of standardized testing, a measure of our achievement as decent human beings.

GOOD
NAKED

"Our policy is brutal honesty."

If You Don't Know Where You Are Going . . .

In the opening chapter, I basically shamed you into letting go of the notion that you need to start your writing project at the beginning. Instead of agonizing over chapter one, I advocated that you dive into a first draft by writing any scene or memory or passage that asserts itself in your consciousness and feels like it might belong somewhere, anywhere, in the story. I promised that this would not set your work on a course for ruin or waste your time—quite the opposite, in fact.

Well, guess what? This same advice pretty much holds up for the entire first draft, whether you are working on a memoir, short fiction, a saga, a cozy mystery, a personal essay, or one of those cookbooks with sweet family stories tethered to each recipe that always make me jealous because my relatives never bonded over Parmesan-crusted zucchini boats.

I love this advice to suspend linearity and chronology for an entire first draft. Instead, focus on accumulating scenic moments in the order in which they beckon you. Write the hot spots—the stuff that feels vivid and demanding of your time now—and figure out later how they flow and fit together. I love this advice because it is both freeing and extremely practical. The freeing part is that it relieves you of the angst of what I call trickle-down plotting, that is, appropriating all your early efforts toward coming up with an overarching structure for your book or essay, with the assumption that it will eventually benefit your characters and afford them opportunities to grow on the page. To paraphrase the International Monetary Fund, the trickle-down theory is whacked. It rarely works to stimulate the economy, and it rarely works to stimulate creativity or productive plotting.

What happens next? We address the void of our empty screens and blank pages. *And, then what? And, then what?*

How the hell should I know? This would be your muse, yelling at you from inside your head, likely because it has had enough of your fretting over structure and plot and what comes next. *Maybe if you gave me a little more to work with, say a bunch of scenes that put your characters on stage and throw in some Roman candles and whiskey, then we could get this party started.*

Clearly, some muses do not do well with writers who wait around to be told what happens in their stories before they write them.

"But what about outlines? If I am going to write a book, shouldn't I follow an outline?"

I do not think I have ever attended a writing conference or workshop where that question has not been raised. I understand the logic of writing from an outline, and I can only imagine the comfort of knowing where you are headed every step of the way. In real life, I have no sense of direction to the degree that if neuro-types took the time to image my cognitive map, I am sure it would look like a crayon scribble from a deranged chimp. Still, while I can empathize with the discomfort of moving forward without a functioning navigation system, my feeling about outlines—specifically related to first drafts—is that they are evil. Pure evil.

This may sound like heresy to all those elementary-grade schoolteachers who rely on the five-paragraph model to help their students organize their thoughts on the page. *Select your thesis topic. Outline your essay into five paragraphs: introduction; supporting paragraph one; supporting paragraph two; supporting paragraph three; and closing or summary paragraph. Now write.* This is indeed a useful model if we are working at a third-grade level, but creating works of literary fiction and narrative nonfiction is not the same as writing an informational essay on when grandma's cat had kittens.

My antipathy toward outlines also runs counter to the advice of one of the biggest-selling authors of all time, James Patterson, who touts the critical importance of outlines in his online master class, "How to Write a Bestseller." I would argue, however, that not everybody writes like James Patterson, which is not necessarily a bad thing.

My feeling is that so many writers ask about outlines because it has been ingrained in us that this is the proper way to proceed, and yet we find creating one next to impossible. Or, if we do manage to come up with an arrangement of plot points and start plugging away, it quickly feels like we are merely connecting the dots, similar to that children's drawing game. This is how boredom can seep into the writing process because, let's face it, once you catch on to the fact that the image you are tracing is a T-Rex, most of the fun of the game is gone.

When I make a point to blaspheme the practice of working from an outline, or writing chapters in the order they are likely to fall, it is not because these methods do not work. Rather, it is because these methods do not work for a lot of writers. And I want the rest of us to respect and cultivate our own non-James-Patterson creative processes, which can also be used to write best sellers. I want us to stop getting hung up on thinking we need to know what comes next, and next, and next . . . and let it go, let it go, let it go.

In *Alice's Adventures in Wonderland*, Lewis Carroll wrote the following exchange between Alice and the Cheshire Cat:

> "Would you tell me, please, which way I ought to go from here?"
>
> "That depends a good deal on where you want to get to," said the Cat.
>
> "I don't much care where—" said Alice.
>
> "Then it doesn't matter which way you go," said the Cat.

"—so long as I get SOMEWHERE," Alice added as an explanation.

"Oh, you're sure to do that," said the Cat, "if you only walk long enough."

This passage has often and aptly been paraphrased, "If you don't know where you are going, any road will get you there." Given that my personal internal navigation system has its own mad logic, I have had to live much of my life by these words, but they also apply to anyone crafting narratives. As writers, we can get there from here in our stories, and it does not matter which road we take, as long as we continue to write until we arrive somewhere.

Look at it this way. A memoirist's work is not just to transcribe his life, but to uncover meaning behind those life experiences for himself, and for his readers. A novelist's work is not just to unfold a series of events, but to explore why her characters do what they do. To engender these types of discoveries and surprises requires that we wander freely in our narratives, or stray from a prescribed path if our attention is called elsewhere. One of my favorite quotes related to this issue is from the science fiction writer Ray Bradbury, who noted in his book *Zen in the Art of Writing*, "Plot is no more than footprints left in the snow after your characters have run by on their way to incredible destinations."

Now is a good time to make an important distinction in narrative craft. The terms *story* and *plot* are often used interchangeably, or at least I use them interchangeably, but it helps to understand how they differ. Story is context. It is a series of events in chronological order. *This happened and then this happened and then this happened.* It is all the stuff that occurred even before the first page of the book. Plot is also a series of events, but plot embodies causality, as in *this happened because that happened.* Here is an example of story: *Geraldine left for work, and then her husband made a spinach and mushroom omelet.* Here's an example of plot: *Geraldine left for work because she couldn't bear to watch her husband make one more spinach and mushroom omelet.* Now that's causality, where emotion and motive drive motion.

I bring up this distinction between story and plot because if we are too wedded to writing in a linear fashion, we often end up with a lot of "and then . . . and then . . . and thens" to show for a hard day's work. Essentially, we get caught up in too much story and not enough plot. The experience is similar to sitting next to someone at a dinner party, who starts out the conversation with the promise, "A funny thing happened on the way to this dinner . . ." But then she goes on to describe how she gets into her car and pulls out of her driveway, but then returns to her house to make sure she's turned off the stove (which she had), and then she gets back in her car and puts on her seat belt and drives to Jiffy Mart to buy a loaf of bread (her daughter likes toast in the morning, sometimes with apple jelly, but not always), and then she hands the cashier a five-dollar bill, and then the cashier gives her change, and then she gets back into her car and goes through town rather than taking the interstate (too much construction!), and then . . .

And then you are ready to fake Guinea worm disease just to escape listening to more of this story. Where is the plot? Where is the funny part?

As a writer, you do not want to feel the need to fake Guinea worm disease when you are working on your own stories. One way to avoid the sensation of plodding through the writing process is to give yourself the freedom to jump around in narrative time and thought. This applies when writing works of any length. The author Charles D'Ambrosio once shared that he writes the first draft of an essay on three-by-five cards, typing sentences or passages in no particular order. This allows him to break "habitual connections . . . and think unlikely thoughts without worry or concern."

From my own experience working with a diversity of writers, I can attest that this nonlinear approach is a much easier way to write for most of us, in that it works with, rather than against, our creative processes. For this reason, I recommend that, even if you already have a sense of order for your story, even if you have outlined your entire narrative arc in James Patterson font, skip ahead on occasion or work on scenes in reverse order. You may also benefit from tossing in something totally random, say an incident that involves your character taking a ride in a hot air balloon decorated with a skull and crossbones, just because you happened to see one that morning hovering over Price Chopper. Now, that would add sizzle to your steak.

Never underestimate the creative fusion derived from the juxtaposition of two unlike or unexpected things. In fact, that element of surprise—often hard to engender through trickle-down plotting—is the very essence of creativity. *Now here's something different*, your neural networks light up. *And just when I thought I was going to have to spend the whole day working on chapter seven, in which my protagonist realizes that he has completed the plot requirements of chapter six, and must now lay the foundation for chapter eight.* Equally important, writing scenes irrespective of order means that you are apt to discover causality in organic, rather than prescribed ways. Your plot will grow as it goes, as your characters, not you, dictate what happens next.

One more point to emphasize the value of a nonlinear creative process. Elmore Leonard famously advised writers, "Leave out the parts people skip." When you focus on writing the scene that calls out to you, rather than the scene that comes next, you avoid spending too much time working on transitions. By transitions, I mean those sections, short or long, that get your characters from here to there. Yet, unless something momentous happens along the way, getting from here to there is counted among the parts people skip.

A lot of authors more trustworthy than I have talked about the importance of discovery and surprise in the writing process. When embarking on the adventure that is storytelling, these writers generously confess that, at least in early drafts, they have no clue how or where a scene fits, or if it even fits at all in a narrative arc. They don't know their beginnings, let alone how the whole thing will turn out. But then, during the writing process, gradually or suddenly a narrative flow—an inevitability—reveals itself that is not just logical, but inspired. That has been the creative process of the majority of people I have worked with over the years who have gone on to complete beautiful short stories, essays, and novels.

But what if I'm not like those other writers, I imagine you may be thinking right now. *What if I write scenes irrespective of order, and they never fit together? Then all I will have are a lot of pages and still no plot.* This, of course, is the big worry, and why we can be so reluctant to let go of the comfort of outlines, even when they give us no comfort. All I can say is that I'm 99.8 percent sure this won't happen to you, because:

1 Whatever scene you decide to write, it is meaningful because it presented itself to you at that moment in time. In addition, if you write the scene that calls out to you, you will skirt a great deal of the potential drudgery of the writing process.

2 Your unconscious is a lot smarter than you, so although your conscious mind may think you are all over the narrative map, one part of you actually knows what it is doing. Even if you write random scenes in any order, you are likely forging connections and creating the elements of a storyline without even being aware of it. The actual flow of that storyline will become clear once you have produced enough scenes to make that structure more readily apparent.

3 Even if 0.2 percent of me can't promise that everything
will turn out just fine, you have no reason to doubt the
wisdom of the Cheshire Cat, whose grin is indicative of a
much more pleasant perspective for navigating the creative
realm. "If you don't know where you are going, any road
will get you there." It just may take a little more time.

Here is a magic trick to keep in your back pocket until you have
accumulated a critical mass of scenes covering different times in
your nascent narrative. Get some note cards, preferably pink because that is my favorite color and serves as a visual reminder
that P is for plot. One to a card, write a shorthand description of
each of your scenes or meaningful moments. (He proposes . . .
She quits her job . . . He sells their dog, and so on) Keep the notes
pithy; you wrote the scenes so you will know what they represent.
Lay the note cards on the floor, or you can tape the cards to a wall,
as long as you use that nonsticky stuff that doesn't leave marks on
the paint. That would drive me crazy. The idea is to get a quick visual overview of the story elements. Now start arranging and rearranging the cards, experimenting with causality. *Maybe this led
to that? No, what if he did this and that made her do that? Yes!* Follow your instincts, which will be sharpened by seeing your scenes
reduced to their essence and laid out spatially before you, rather
than in consecutive pages.

This spatial exercise is a thing of wonder. I have used it myself, and when I witness others doing this exercise on the orange
striped rug of my writer's center, I swear I can almost see the note
cards rising from the floor and rearranging themselves, revealing
a movement far more inspired than any order our consciousness
could have imposed. A narrative arc, a storyline, an inevitability
always manifests. As if you had planned it. As if it was there all
along. Of course the flow is not perfect. Of course this newly revealed structure has lumps and bumps, holes to be filled, scenes

to be sacrificed. But holy smokes, what you have achieved is a solid first draft. And with that in hand, now would be a good time to actually write yourself an outline, if you still feel the need. Just be careful to leave plenty of space between the dots to allow for a few more surprises.

Good Naked

Like so many television shows today, the one I was watching on my laptop featured an ensemble cast of good-looking men and women at the top of their games—brilliant lawyers, world leaders, rainmakers, and other speed-talkers who, pretty much to a one, were also murderers or accomplices to murder. In this latest episode, I had just witnessed the President of the United States smother a homicidal Supreme Court Justice with a pillow. This was disturbing, to be sure, but it was not until my show was interrupted by a commercial for one of those after-school learning centers that I felt truly shocked.

The ad featured a smiling Indian boy, twelve years old, though he looked a bit younger in his striped t-shirt.

"So far, I have taken eleven college courses. Those courses were either physics, calculus, or chemistry." The boy spoke somewhat formally, whether it was because English was his second language or because his youth had been exorcised. A montage of shots showed him concave over a school desk, doing computations on worksheets, and then scrolling through code on a computer screen. A friendly voice-over explained how the center's learning method is designed to put your children ahead of their peers in math and reading.

I did a computer search to check out the center's other promotions. There was little Christine, age ten, sporting a big bow in her shiny black hair cut in a pageboy. "I went to Johns Hopkins and I took a geometry class." Christine spoke directly into the camera. "Right now I am learning about different square roots and we are doing the Pythagorean theory!"

Seriously. From the mouths of babes, a theorem stating that the square of the length of the hypotenuse of a right triangle is equal to the sum of the squares of the lengths of the other sides. Maybe, I thought, Christine needed such a big bow to keep her head from exploding.

Another spot from a different campaign for the learning center opened with a little girl leaping from a diving platform miles above the pool below. The voice-over promised parents their children would develop learning skills that would make them fearless in school and beyond. The girl, maybe six, looked thrilled in her midair close-up, but the message, as I interpreted it, was, "Hey, Slacker Mom! Why isn't your first grader jumping from dizzying heights?"

I had always thought these types of learning centers were in the business of tutoring kids who needed help catching up academically with their classmates, but what the ads made clear was their real purpose, which is to create adorable androids capable of overtaking the world.

For the record, I am not a slacker, and my children are perfect. But this mentality—that a kid should be ahead of his or her peers—feels wrong to me. What is the problem with being where you should be, when you are there? After all, a peer is someone who, by definition, is at your own level; the word comes from the Latin par, which means equal. So if you are a twelve-year-old boy, what is wrong with being equal to other twelve-year-old boys? Of course, like every stage of kidhood, this one comes with issues. Wouldn't we like all children to skip the age where they are incapable of throwing out empty wrappers? That aside, why rush it? Why not appreciate every stage of development for its unique, age-appropriate attributes, and trust that derivatives will come along all too soon?

I think a lot writers share this mindset, that their kids should be advanced well beyond their peers. Only it is not our actual kids we feel this way about, but rather another form of progeny, our creative work, which, similar to children, also matures in stages. This is known as the drafting process, and is as certain a course of development as infancy is followed by childhood, followed by adolescence, followed by adulthood. Yet often we fault our first drafts for not being more mature, say more like a final draft. We hope for shortcuts, and think we should be able to skip stages, but this is not how stories and poems evolve and reach their potential. Indeed, trying to hurry things along rarely ends well. Not just in academics, but in other realms as well. Just look at all those former child stars who grow up to be troubled adults. Just look at those bedazzled toddlers in beauty pageants. Let these examples serve as warnings. Your first draft does not need a tiara. And thinking it does only puts you in danger of becoming one of those obnoxious stage parents whose pushy behavior is likely to leave you and your creative process mentally scarred for life.

For some people, me for one, the first draft is the hardest to produce. Sometimes I wish I could hire someone to write it for me and spare me a lot of anxiety and stress eating. *I got nothing*, I think, the thought reinforced by a blank page staring back at me. Of course this is not true; I have got plenty, as do you if you happen to feel similarly when confronting what feels like the creative void. The real issue is not that you lack ideas, but rather that you lack access to those ideas. In addition, the challenge is to single out the material that matters to you now: the story or memory or scene at the front of the line, pushing against the velvet rope between your unconscious and conscious. To tap into your most urgent material, you simply need to manufacture an *in*, which often means seizing on the first thing that pops into your mind or line of vision—the last birthday present your character received, or the bobblehead on your boss's desk that looks remarkably like him. This practice of writing "outside your story" may seem like a loopy way to find your in, but weirdly enough it works to quickly steer you in the direction of relevant content. Or not. Regardless, as Flannery O'Connor once said, "Not-writing is a good deal worse than writing." So there's that.

Accessing your story material is but one challenge related to first drafts. Another is the chorus of critics in your head who tsk-tsk and shush you every time you type something questionable, for example, the letter A. Some writers must deal with a lot of tsk-tskers and shushers inside their heads. Mine, however, is a chorus of one, the Empress Dourager (pronounced like Dowager), who is basically me, grown more imperious with each passing year I have worked as a writing instructor and professional editor. I start to type, something, anything: *There was a dog in the yard . . .*

"How many times," asks the Empress Dourager, adjusting her silk robes embroidered with dragons, "have you told your very own writing students that *There was* is a weak construction?"

I delete my first effort and try again: *A dog sits in the yard.*

"A dog?" The Empress Dourager has one of her eunuchs point to the offending sentence and hold his nose. "I take this to mean you were lying all those times you told your students about the importance of *specific* detail?"

A corgi sits . . .

"Corgis are vile!" The Empress Dourager slices the air with one of her six-inch gold filigreed fingernail covers.

A Pekinese . . .

"A Pekinese!" the Empress Dourager shrieks, and another eunuch instantly appears with a perfect specimen of the breed, bedecked in gems and bows. "What entitles you, one of the Worthless Unworthies, to dare to write about a Pekinese?"

On a good writing day, this is when I might catch myself and realize how ridiculous it is to listen to someone who uses the phrase "Worthless Unworthies." Still, the Empress Dourager is why it can sometimes take me forever to achieve a first draft.

If you also struggle in this early phase of the creative process, it can be helpful to employ mental strategies to silence your internal critics, and thus alleviate the fear and paralysis that prevent us from outwitting the blank page. In her popular book for writers, *Bird by Bird*, Anne Lamott has a chapter titled "Shitty First Drafts." She advises people like us to think of our early efforts in these terms, as a way to free ourselves from the pressure of high expectations. If we accept, even own the fact that our first draft is going to be shitty, we may be less inclined to second-guess ourselves, and more accepting of whatever mess we make on the page.

I remember loving Anne Lamott's book when I read it years ago. That said, I never liked the concept of shitty first drafts. For starters, I don't want to write shit. Not even in a first draft. This does not mean I expect beautifully structured stories to flow through my chipped fingernails, though wouldn't that be a lovely miracle. In fact, my first drafts typically are an accumulation of random musings, scenic fragments, and rants at people I am too intimidated to confront in real life. Still, I need to believe I have more going on than a poo-throwing chimp at the zoo. But what really bothers me about the concept of shitty first drafts is the idea of labeling this stage of the creative process in such derogatory terms. Though a first draft may be miles from polished prose or poetry, it is also far from crap, and calling it ugly names only makes it that much harder for the writer to recognize its merits.

In my workshops, participants have no place to hide. Students are expected to read aloud from their work every week, including first drafts. Almost to a one, they preface their reading with an apology.

"I'm sorry this is so bad."

"Ugh, the beginning of this chapter doesn't even make sense. And I don't have a clue where it's going."

"Okay, I'll read what I wrote, but it really sucks."

I understand why writers resist sharing unpolished drafts. I don't even like going to the gym without lip gloss. Regardless, this is a workshop, meaning my point is not to shame participants by outing their mismatched tenses and other editorial weaknesses, but rather to shed light on craft and the creative process. Think of it as the difference between good naked and bad naked. When you are in a low-lit bathroom enjoying a steamy shower, for example, with your glossy curves as inviting as a seal pup's, that is good naked. Whereas later, when you are still damp and trying to squeeze into your control-top underwear, that is bad naked. Sharing your early drafts is good naked. Yes, you are exposed, but there is your creative process in all its shining glory.

Sometimes one of the apologists in a workshop will read what she wrote from, say, a fifteen-minute writing exercise, and the piece will be astounding—an entire story gracefully unfolded in a narrative arc, captured in concrete detail and metaphoric images, and resonating with thematic significance. How did she do that? The other group members and I shake our heads in wonder, while the writer herself looks bemused. The only explanation is the magic that can happen when writing from a prompt. You, me, the retired postal worker who only signed up for the class because his wife wanted him out of her kitchen—we are all capable of this kind of magic, given the right incantation, mood, and moment. But as this apologist demonstrates, most of us are initially blind to the merits of our own work, simply because we wrote it. Keep this in mind to avoid prematurely trashing a draft, figuratively and literally. (Also keep in mind that if you do dash off a brilliant writing exercise, the next person in line to read will hate you, but in a good way.) Though brilliant writing occurs more freakishly than one might expect in a first draft, more typical is that someone will share an early effort—whether the result of a timed writing exercise or weeks of forced effort—and the piece will reflect something quite different: words on the page that mark a beginning.

Let's pick on an easy target in first drafts: adverbs. As Stephen King once said, "The road to hell is paved with adverbs." Elmore Leonard also warned that to use an adverb in almost any way is a "mortal sin."

To emphasize the evils of adverbs, some writing instructors forbid their students to use them, even in first drafts. I am not a fan of adverbs any more than these teachers, but I think that rule serves only as one more barrier between the writer and a healthy creative process. A first draft is the one place where we should feel free to happily, defiantly, gluttonously toss in adverbs. Later, these modifiers may be vilified as Satan's spawn, but in a first draft they make great placeholders. They capture the gist of what we want to say without slowing us down by figuring out how to say it in just the right way. Consider the following:

Suddenly, he decided to tell her she needed to move out!!!

What is wrong with that sentence? You could answer, just about everything. The three-syllable adverb "suddenly" undermines its own meaning. The use of indirect rather than direct dialogue fails to convey the intensity of the protagonist's feelings. The sentence is all telling and no showing. And the reasons not to use an exclamation point, let alone three, are obvious!!!

On the other hand, you could say that sentence rocks. Because now the writer has a first draft that captures his intentions. And there that adverb-y sentence will wait, doing the important work of holding that thought until the writer sees his way through to some kind of end, and can then revise accordingly.

Suddenly, he decided to tell her she needed to move out!!!
He decided she needed to move out!!

She needed to move out!

"Leave."

Earlier today in our workshop, one writer shared a draft that jumped from yellow apples decaying on the lawn, to a wooden trunk in an attic, to a shackled prisoner telling a loved one that he is dying of cancer. The writer didn't want to read the parts about the apples on the lawn or the trunk in the attic because the story found its foothold in the tension and immediacy of the prison scene. She was right to recognize that her meandering opening didn't serve as a good beginning, but those lead-in paragraphs beautifully revealed the way our creative minds are always at work, finding patterns and connections and meaning through unconscious devices like free association and repetition. At this stage of the process, our hardest job as sentient beings is simply to stop thinking and get out of our own way.

In the same workshop, we also reviewed another early draft where the narrative flatlined for several pages, thanks to a long, expository block of backstory. But that section taught the writer a good deal about her protagonist, and if divvied up and sized appropriately, the information likely will serve other scenes throughout the story.

The class also considered the first draft of an essay in which the writer raced us through a meaningful personal experience at the pace of a spooked horse. But with the achievement of this draft, he can now mine the material for what I call "hot spots," those key moments worthy of scenic development.

This is why I push writers to share their early drafts. This is why there is no need to apologize for the fact that a first draft is not a final draft. We spend so much time hoping to discover the secret of how to write more effectively and expeditiously. I think the answer is right there on the pages in front of us. The answer is revealed in each and every draft, from the first to the last. How do we access our muse? A first draft can show us, if we aren't too distracted by calling it names. How do we get from here to there? Look! There is the creative process, all mapped out for us draft by draft (by draft by draft).

Not too long ago, a woman in one of my workshops said something that made me rethink my own difficulty confronting a blank page. She came to the group with a scene she'd been struggling to write for quite a while. Before she started reading aloud, she said, "This is a predraft so it's really holey." I am sure what she meant was that the piece was full of holes, but her words struck me in a different way. What I heard was "holy," as in sacred. Holy, as in highly valued and important, deserving of great respect.

That was when it really hit home that writers need to honor every draft. We need to respect even our predrafts. We need to recognize the value of every stage of the development of our manuscripts because if we don't, we are always going to be apologizing, and are likely to overlook the crucial role that every draft serves in the creative process. A first draft is not a blank page. A third draft paves the way for a fourth draft. A penultimate draft illuminates those tiny missed opportunities that can elevate our work to its highest level.

Many times, I have heard people say, "I don't like writing but I like the fact that I've written." This feels wrong to me on so many levels, which only makes it worse because sometimes I feel this way too. As working writers, our entire job description is to create drafts. This is where we spend all our time. So if we do not find meaning and merit in the *now* of the creative process, if we are always wishing for a draft more advanced than the one we are working on in the moment, then our writing lives will always be devoid of joy, until all of the work is done.

I try to remind myself of this when facing that dreaded empty screen. *This is a predraft*, I remind myself, *so it is really holy*. Even when my words still don't flow easily, sometimes this actually helps. Sometimes it silences the Empress Dourager long enough for me to appreciate the total freedom that is unique, even sacred to this early stage of the creative process. I have already made it clear in this chapter that thinking in terms of a shitty first draft has never inspired me when I sit down to work. But I can tell you one thing as a writer who wants to keep writing: nothing is more motivating to me than not wanting to feel like shit.

Can I Be Honest?

The other day I bought nail clippers for the cat. When I got them home, I happened to read the descriptive copy on the back: "Double-bladed guillotine trimmer." What? I just wanted to trim the kitty's nails, not behead him.

Maybe the manufacturer was simply being technically accurate. Maybe a "double-bladed guillotine" is the generic term for any pet product that snips off the pointy tip of a cat's toenail. I have my suspicions, however, that the copywriter who came up with that product description was either (a) deeply disturbed, or (b) aiming for overkill, as a way to convince consumers that this product means business. Everyone knows how cats hate to get their nails trimmed, so you can believe, gentle consumer, that any device described as a double-bladed guillotine is going to make short work of the job and show your cat who is boss.

We live in a violent world. We are surrounded by violent images in the news and at the cinemaplex. A consensus of studies claim that all this ugliness in our environment definitely has an impact, similar to the correlation between secondhand smoke and the risk of lung cancer. Say you are a kid in the seventies. You and your two older sisters are enshrouded in the nicotine cloud that is the back seat of your family's Buick sedan.

"She touched me!"

"She touched me first!"

Thankfully, not every kid raised in such toxicity will develop lung cancer, but the absence of proven causality does not mean that one thing doesn't lead to the other, or that my sister did not touch me first. With so much anger and ugliness and aggression in the world, it is virtually impossible not to be affected by it all on some level. Even when we try to shield ourselves from the horrors of what humans are capable of, violence insinuates itself into our worldview, our language, even our most banal thoughts.

I'd kill for a mango smoothie.

Take that last parking space and you're a dead man.

I do not mean to suggest that thinking such thoughts implies a criminally insane personality, especially because both of those examples recently came from my own head. No one—well, no one except Biblical literalists—is that ridiculously concrete. But I do think it would not hurt for me, and perhaps other people wound as tightly as me, to think about the effects our everyday expressions of violence have on ourselves and others. Do I really want to risk the chance that I might be perceived as the kind of person who contemplates murder in exchange for a tropical refreshment, or to avoid having to walk an extra block to my cardio class? What's more, like the double-sided guillotine that is my cat's nail trimmer, a violent metaphor can cut two ways. Yes, it can set a tone—*I mean business*—but it can also set a course for cruelty, however unintentional.

Consider the use of the term *brutal honesty* in the feedback interaction.

"Here's my manuscript, Charlotte. Don't bother being nice. I want you to be brutally honest."

Writers use that expression a lot. And by a lot, I mean almost every writer who is sincere about improving his or her work has probably demanded brutal honesty at one time or another from a writing group, a grandma (the nice one), or a reader-at-large. In the writing realm, this call for brutal honesty serves as shorthand for implying the following message: "I am serious about my work. I neither need nor want to be coddled." In essence, when writers put out the call for brutal honesty, they are encouraging feedback providers to be cruel to be kind, to trash their work for the sake of art.

Whenever I hear a writer, or people in the real world for that matter, insisting on brutal honesty, I feel the need to download a cute animal video to calm down. It doesn't matter how serious the writer is about wanting to learn craft. It doesn't matter if she has the kind of fortitude that has allowed her to shatter the glass ceiling, or serve in the armed forces, or host pool parties for her sixth grader's entire class, or all three at once. Any feedback interaction that starts out with a demand for savagery, which is the definition of brutality, is at worst going to devastate the recipient, or at best leave the person feeling bemused. *What just happened? Is it me, or is that guy an asshole?*

Brutality has no place in any educational interaction. By insisting on brutal honesty (who originally paired those words, Vlad the Impaler?) we may think we are setting the stage for a more productive interaction, but we are actually doing the opposite. In effect, we are cornering our readers into being nothing but negative, and that is not pleasant for either party. When a writing client demands from me brutal honesty, I am almost afraid to offer any feedback that does not go for the jugular for fear that the writer will think I am a liar, or a softie, or one of those readers who don't have a clue that "harrumphed" is a terrible dialogue tag. When put in this position, cornered into savagery, this is my internal monologue: *How dare he assume that I need help giving feedback! How dare he mistrust the value of my non-brutal opinions, as if saying something nice is a sign of my ineptitude!* And then, thoroughly worked up about this call for brutality, it takes all my professional acumen to just do my job as a writing instructor, which is partly to tell the writer what is working in the stupid story so that he can write forward productively.

Equally counterproductive is when a writer demands brutal honesty from his workshop peers because even an evolved group is likely to comply. We all have baser instincts just waiting to be tapped, and once one feedback provider opts for brutality, watch out.

"I stopped reading at page two."

"I doubt if any editor is going to care about your kid's weird medical condition."

"If you are going to inflict your writing on us, then at least stick to blogging."

An invitation to brutality opens the door to vague, dismissive, lazy pronouncements like these. Though the writer's intent is to direct the conversation toward meaningful insights, what she really is doing is giving her readers an out from the actual work that goes into providing constructive criticism. Here, let me be clear: brutal honesty and constructive criticism are not synonymous. Brutal honesty requires an unmitigated harshness, whereas constructive criticism takes an awareness of EQ, that is, the emotional quotient that factors into successful educational and interpersonal exchanges. Often, writers are taken by surprise at how much EQ matters to them when receiving feedback. Consider the following anecdote from my well-balanced and talented friend Kendra, who represents countless other well-balanced and talented writers out there who think they have no use for EQ. "The very first time I was in a workshop, I wanted 'real' feedback, by which I meant the good and the bad. The people in the workshop certainly gave me both, but there were not many ground rules in place about how to give feedback. Honestly," Kendra added, "I don't think the people were very mean that day; I had just never gotten any negative feedback at all face to face. I rode my bike home nearly blind, crying all the way."

It's bad enough that brutal honesty is, well, brutal, but it also steals the attention from positive feedback, and how this force for good plays a vital role in the educational interaction. A lot of writers confuse positive feedback with flattery, but the difference is significant. Positive feedback educates the recipient. It is mean-ingful praise because it is backed by authenticating detail that il-luminates what is working in a manuscript and, most important, why it works. Positive feedback underscores effective uses of craft through examples in the writer's own work, which bolsters under-standing and self-confidence. In addition, it offers the writer a much-needed perspective during the revision process. When we are too close to our work to tease out the good from the bad, posi-tive feedback helps guide our judgment so we do not second-guess what should not be disturbed. Lastly, sincere positive feedback makes the recipient feel good, which is a lovely thing for the be-stower as well, unless of course you are a pinchy, jealous-type person.

Recently, I was complaining in my evening workshop about a writer in my daytime class who, despite my longstanding and oft-repeated ban of the use of that phrase in class, still insisted her fellow participants be brutally honest when discussing her sub-mission. I respect this writer because she has worked hard to ac-quire craft and revise her manuscript accordingly, and because she is not shy about wearing thigh-high boots to a Vermont work-shop full of felt clogs. I know that she insisted on brutality be-cause she would rather join an underfunded circus than write a bad novel. Plus, like so many workshop participants—newbies and seasoned—she gets anxious when her work is about to be discussed, and this call for brutal honesty is an obvious psycho-logical defense mechanism. *If I insist on the worst-case scenario, I'll be better prepared to handle it.* Still, with so much awfulness in the outside world, to open the door to brutality in the warm, safe, productive environment of my writer's center felt like sacrilege.

"Why can't writers let go of that stupid choice of words?" I asked the members of my evening workshop, who had been around me long enough to know that this was a rhetorical question, and that they were about to get an earful. It is not uncommon for me to get worked up about phraseology. Take another expression that drives me crazy—"It's just a matter of semantics." People often say this as a dismissive ploy in an argument. Essentially, the comment is a way to shut up the other person by implying, *we're basically saying the same thing*. But that is a ridiculous contortion of logic, because semantics are about meaning, so an argument is all about semantics; there is no "just" about it. And if the argument is not about meaning, and the two parties truly are saying the same thing, then why are they arguing in the first place?

You see. This is how I get riled up about certain matters of lexical units. Still, as I listened to myself rant about the ridiculous call for brutal honesty in human interactions, writerly or otherwise, I wondered if part of my strong reaction had to do with my own defense mechanisms. Maybe I was making too much out of a figure of speech? Maybe I was being hypersensitive, like those pit bull owners who get bent out of shape just because you won't let their dog lick your baby's face. On the other hand, even though my opinion about that phrase was just that—my opinion—I knew I was right.

"The next time someone demands 'brutal honesty' in one of my workshops," I snapped, "they owe me ten bucks!" Then I thought better of this rash demand. "No, they owe me twenty bucks, plus a bottle of top-shelf vermouth!"

"The other week, I was telling my aunt about your positive approach to feedback," one of the group members interjected. This was a participant who had attended many of my classes over the years, a family doctor who crafts beautiful short stories and is unfazed by ugly eruptions. He went on to explain that his octogenarian Aunt Liv lives in Manhattan, and has been meeting with the same small group of writers for almost four decades, some of whom are widely published and known for their social and political activism. "I told my aunt how supportive we are in your workshops," he shared, "and that it's nice."

Here we go, I thought, feeling even more defensive. I figured I was about to hear how some rabble-rousing senior from the big city had deemed me the Rebecca of Sunnybrook Farm among writing teachers.

"So, what did your Aunt Liv say when you told her about our 'nice' workshop?" I made myself ask.

"Nothing much at first," he answered. "She was quiet for a few moments, but then she said something that really surprised me."

In the brief pause that followed, I started replaying all the arguments I have heard through the years from people who disparage positive feedback and the value of a supportive workshop:

"Writers need to toughen up!"

"Why encourage people who don't have any talent?"

"If a person can't handle someone ripping apart their work, they aren't cut out to be a writer."

The family doctor interrupted my thoughts. "I hate my writing group," he said. "That was what my aunt said to me after I told her how much I like our workshop."

Whoa.

I did not quite trust what I had heard, so I asked him to tell me her words verbatim.

"I hate my writing group," he repeated. "Those were her exact words."

Now that, I thought, is brutal honesty, especially coming from a woman who has shared her creative life with these fellow writers for decades. In fact, her response felt so brutally honest to me that, for once, I found myself at a loss for words, too surprised and sad to say then what I will say now to anyone who has ever used or defended that ridiculously cruel phrase—"I told you so."

The Reverse Curse

In Australian Aboriginal culture, there is a practice known as bone pointing, intended to bring sickness or death to someone, often as punishment for a crime. The ritual is conducted by a learned man assigned great spiritual power. He wears special shoes made from bird feathers, and carries a bone, typically a kangaroo femur, about nine inches long with a pointed tip and endowed with magical powers by having curses sung or muttered over it. The victim has no idea when the Bone Pointer will come for him, until this great spiritual power sneaks up and makes his presence known. He points the bone in the victim's direction, but never touches him directly. Regardless, the condemned man knows he has been cursed and will surely die. Then he does. It may take a few weeks, maybe a month for him to waste away, but the outcome is assured. To point the bone at someone is akin to killing him with black magic.

Inside almost every writer's head is a Bone Pointer. Some internal sorcerer, some part of ourselves we have vested with the power of killing our writing dreams. Our Bone Pointers may not require the use of anything as exotic as the femur of an unfortunate kangaroo, but their black magic is just as formidable. They have only to sneak up on our psyches, make sure we know they are standing there in their fancy birdie shoes, and curse our writing ambitions. From that point forward, fear quickly begins to lay waste to our future. Fear of failure. Fear of success. Fear of exposure. Fear of making a mistake. Fear of finishing. Fear of letting go. Whatever form the fear takes, the outcome is the same. Once we ascribe power to the Bone Pointer and he works his psychological voodoo, our ability to finish the work we started is doomed, and this without anyone even laying a hand on our manuscripts.

As a writing teacher, I like to think that craft is the only thing that stands between you and me and the writing we want to accomplish. With craft, we can make up for any deficits in talent. In fact, talent is a concept I would just as soon ignore, given that it can do more mischief than service. Often, talent can't be bothered to step in while the aspiring artist makes a bit of a fool of herself during the learning process, for example, by trying to emulate the style of a famous author. *It is a truth universally acknowledged, that a writer in possession of an imitative style must be in want of her own voice.*

Maybe your talent thinks this is funny, to emerge later in life, after you have endured years of eye rolling and rejection.

"Surprise!" it shouts, as your own writing voice finally emerges and you land on material suitable to your strengths. "See there, you aren't as creatively challenged as your sophomore English teacher would have had you believe."

Equally vexing is when your talent reveals itself right from the get-go, but then has no real interest in working a desk job. And why would it, when it can be out on the town, wined and dined as the darling among lesser talents?

"When can we expect to see a finished copy of that fabulous book of yours?" your former workshop peers, your agent, your parents who are still bankrolling you all ask with eagerness.

"I'm just waiting for the manuscript to finish writing itself," your talent quips back, reinforcing your reputation as a master of dry wit. The only problem is, one part of your talent actually believes this fantasy, while another part is busy rummaging through your pockets hoping to find a loose Xanax.

All this is to say, talent is not the most reliable arbiter of who will find success and happiness as a writer. Yes, some people have a better ear for language, a greater gift for storytelling, while others have to work really, really hard to acquire narrative techniques and layer them into their work, draft after draft. Thankfully, however, craft evens the playing field for most of us. In fact, if I had to put money on which writers in a group were most likely to succeed, I would go with the hardest workers, those students who have to endure instructors like me repeating over and over that mixed metaphors (*His eyes bore into her like granite headstones melting her wooden soul*) aren't doing their work any favors. These group members revise, return with stronger drafts, and then endure more constructive criticism, to tackle other editorial issues:

"Dialogue is not conversation. Make it more pithy . . ."

"Description, even gorgeous description, must never be allowed to disrupt the narrative flow . . ."

"What do you mean, *She thought to herself*? Who else would she be thinking to?"

And so on and on, until eventually these hardworking, craft acquiring, maybe-talented-maybe-not-talented-but-it-doesn't-matter-either-way writers end up with a final draft of a beautiful story that works on every level, and I get to celebrate my success at being such a good teacher.

Given my faith in the creative process, not to mention my outsized ego as an instructor, I sometimes can sound flip, or reductive, when aspiring authors ask me how to go about writing their books.

"One scene after another," I tell them, "then just slap on some craft." As far as an overview of the writing process goes, I actually think this is pretty good advice, and my breezy tone is only intended to serve as a reminder that we should not assign too much preciousness to the job. Later, over cocktails at the book launch party, we can talk about muses and the mystical mysteries of literary achievement, after the work is all done.

"One scene after another, then just slap on some craft." I repeat this refrain in every workshop, at every conference where I speak, and in my own head when I sit down to write. "That's how you get the job done and achieve your writing dreams."

As sound as I believe this advice to be, the reality is that it has not served all of my former students in the longer run, including some of the best writers I know. For these folks, craft is not enough, or rather craft is not the issue. In fact, a good many of these people have craft to spare, plus a great deal of talent, plus minds so sharp I suspect that their brains have brains of their own. And yet their book projects wither in their desk drawers. These writers cannot bring themselves to complete their perfectly viable works, and the reasons for this defy all explanation but one: the Bone Pointer in their heads has made his presence known.

To understand how bad this situation feels—though I suspect most of us already know—consider the zero-sum hand game Rock-Paper-Scissors. In case you need a refresher, at the count of three, two players simultaneously thrust out a hand in the form of one those objects. (A fist represents rock, a flat hand symbolizes paper, and two fingers in the shape of a V indicate scissors.) The rules of winning the game are straightforward: rock crushes scissors; scissors cut paper; and paper covers rock, though this last one has always seemed a bit of a stretch to me. Given that each object has a unique advantage over one of the others, every game results in a different winner and loser, unless of course there is a tie, in which case the game continues for another round.

Now let's play the writing version of this game, except this version swaps out Rock-Paper-Scissors for three different entities: Craft-Talent-Fear. Are you ready to play? One, two, three . . .

Fear wins over craft.

Fear wins over talent.

Fear always wins.

It doesn't matter which object your hand forms—when you are up against fear, the outcome is always the same.

A psychiatrist friend once told me a bit of wisdom his advisor shared with him years ago during his residency. "As a psychiatrist, all you can legitimately expect from patients is that they pay their bills." At first, this sounded like a cop-out, especially considering the fact that the patient is likely paying $150 per fifty-minute hour. But then my friend went on to explain: you can't expect any more than that because otherwise it means your ego is tied up in whether the patient gets better or worse, and that would be assigning yourself too much credit or blame. As a doctor, you can try to do your best, but the ultimate outcome is in the hands of the patient, or God, or the weather.

I have come to understand why this is sound advice for psychi atrists, and probably for everybody else in the world. In the end, we are all responsible for ourselves, so let's keep our egos out of other people's problems. As a writing instructor, however, it goads me to see sincere writers struggling, and books that deserve to be finished left to fester in file cabinets. I want to fix the situation, to throw solutions at the writer until one of them sticks or the person takes out a restraining order. I know this contradicts a common complaint women have about men—*Otis, I'm not asking you to fix my problem; I just need you to listen while I talk*. But in this dynamic, I side with Otis. *Let's just solve the problem, and then I will listen to you talk about your feelings, if I am still awake.*

All this is to say, I really wish I knew what to do when writers fail to finish the worthy works they have started. Here, I am not talking about someone who has simply lost interest in the form —"Ah, this writing business, what a waste of energy. It's time I tried my hand at fiber art." I am talking about the award-winning journalist who wowed my workshop with his chapters, but could not overcome his perfectionism to finalize the last draft of his richly textured novel. (Note: perfectionism is an affliction, not an indicator of owning more editorial integrity than other writers. It only avoids the real issue when we presume completion equates to compromise.) I am talking about one of my colleagues in academia, a creative force in several languages, who tried to transform her dissertation into a trade book, but gave up in the final stretch and subsequently was denied tenure. I am talking about another writing teacher and professional freelancer who has used the excuse of her cluttered desk to explain why she still hasn't completed the very marketable memoir she started back in the nineties.

I feel for these writers. I feel for them because I know ambushed ambitions like these can niggle you for the rest of your life, or they can tear you up inside. And the longer the fear lingers, the stronger its grip. As one writer who is struggling to finish the beautiful memoir she has been working on for years recently told me, "I'm either going to finish my book or suicide. At this point it could go either way."

One time, I met a friend—who has been avoiding his partially finished manuscript of a historical novel for years—at a local pub for drinks. Two ales later he said to me, "A lot of us talk about writing our books, but you're someone who actually does it." I almost spewed my IPA. Plenty of times, I have abandoned personally meaningful projects for no reason other than fear. Indeed, even as my friend and I chatted, I could sense my own Bone Pointer nearby, whittling to a sharp point the end of some poor animal's femur, just waiting to sneak up on me when I exited the ladies' room or headed to my Prius.

Still, my friend's comment stuck with me, and made me think about what I have done—the techniques and tricks I have called on through the years—to overcome my fear, at least for long enough intervals to see some books through to completion.

One trick I have used involves impulse control, or lack of. Even in the throes of fear, I still experience random moments of courage. No, courage is too noble a word; the feeling is more like a burst of temper, a flare of defiance—*I am so sick of feeling lousy about not working on my book! I am so sick of not believing I can do this.* So I capitalize on that feeling of frustration and now-or-never urgency. In one case, I picked up the phone and called the press that had published one of my previous books.

"I have another book idea," I shouted at the unfamiliar editor on the other end of the line (my previous editor had left the press years earlier). Are you interested? Can I send you a proposal, right now, so you can take a look?"

"Um, what was your name again?" the editor asked.

Yes, I know all about the importance of professional decorum and making a good first impression. I have attended plenty of publishing panels where editors and agents underscore these virtues. They warn their audience not to ambush them with cold calls or dash off sloppily rendered queries and proposals. And who can argue? We are, after all, supposed to be mature. But I would rather risk being hung up on, or send off an email query with a typo, than miss those fleeting moments when fear gives way to opportunity. In fact, at one of these very same conferences, I ignored impulse control once again, and approached one of the editor panelists to pitch a work-in-progress.

"I'm completing a collection of essays," I said, referring to a project that, at the time, felt like a pipe dream in a clogged sewer line. Though I had been working on these personal essays for quite some time, my Bone Pointer took every opportunity to remind me that no one cares about my little stories of life, love, and neurotic human behavior. "I think my voice and themes are a good match for your press," I heard my impulsive self assert with false confidence, "and so I would like to send you a few pieces for consideration."

"Fine," the editor said, whether it was because I seemed authorial or unstable, I'll never know. Regardless, her "fine" was just enough encouragement to dodge my Bone Pointer long enough to complete the collection and see the book through to publication.

You may not be willing or ready to phone a publishing house out of the blue, or corner an editor at a writing conference, but there are other impulsive acts you can do to elude your own Bone Pointer. Why not sit down right now and write a query to an agent, to make your work feel more real? If your manuscript is far enough along, send the query off. What the heck. And if that agent is not interested, well, you will have made progress in the meantime, and can send out another query to keep you on task. If dealing with agents is not of interest or premature, then sign up for a writing class in your community or online. Do it this week. No more procrastination. No more excuses. Tricks like this may seem goofy—Real writers just sit down and write! Except that they don't. Almost every successful author I know plays some kind of head game to keep writing, or to shake off a funk. Think about the ways you have motivated yourself to complete other challenging tasks throughout your life. Ask around to see how your writer friends keep on keeping on—whether it is by manufacturing a deadline, lining up a reader for accountability, or denying themselves chocolate until meeting a 500-words-a-day quota. Not every trick works for every writer, but once you find one that serves you, it can make a big difference.

Therapists who work with people on overcoming a fear of failure, or a fear of success, or whatever you want to call the fear that thwarts us from achieving our goals, explain that part of the challenge is that these kinds of fears relate to the future. But the future does not exist, so how do we change it? The first step is to pinpoint what exactly it is that scares us. To do so, psychologists recommend a method called visualization, creating a detailed picture of the future as we imagine it. What does success or failure look like in your future? Once your book is done, will your life fall apart? Will your relatives suddenly want to borrow money? Will your book club choose your work to discuss at its next meet-

ing, and then tear it apart? Or, what if you don't manage to finish your work? What does that look like? Maybe the scene in *Les
Misérables* where Fantine sings "I Dreamed a Dream." Regardless,
with your fear visualized, you are better able to confront it directly and create an alternative future.

I can understand how this trick of visualization works. In fact,
I realized I had been unknowingly practicing this technique for
quite some time. Only, I did not just see my worst fear realized
in my mind's eye, I actually had it taped to the door of my own
writer's center. The image is captured in a *New Yorker* cartoon by
Gahan Wilson that shows a tombstone with the epitaph "George
Appleton Harvey. 1928–2003. He never got around to writing
that novel."

Visualizing our fear is one step toward overcoming it, or at
least skirting it for a bit. Psychologists also recommend going a
step further: not just manifesting mental images of the things that
scare us, but then destroying those images in our imagination.
This actually sounds like fun, like playing those senselessly violent video games, only without the misogyny and with a point.
With that in mind, I think we should all take a moment to do
the following creative visualization, or as I like to think of it—a
reverse curse.

Imagine the Bone Pointer in your head. Make him vivid, like
the characters you are writing about in your book. What is he
doing? My Bone Pointer is slouched on the couch, watching an
episode about "Manic Mom Makeovers" on *The Doctors*. He does
not see me hiding behind the ficus. I suspect your Bone Pointer is
equally clueless. Sneak up behind him. Slowly, slowly. Get close
enough that you can reach out and touch his comb-over, but do
not lay a hand on him.

"Hey, Feather Feet!" Shout this at the top of your lungs. Watch
your Bone Pointer leap off the couch. He is so startled, his bird
booties instantly molt.

"Don't scare me like that," your Bone Pointer whines.

"Oh, puh-leeze." You hand him his eyeglasses, which had fallen on the floor when he jumped in fright. The nosepiece is held together with black electrical tape. "What about all those days, weeks, months, years you scared me with your silly curses and nasty pointing?" You say this not to make fun of his culture, but to make your point clear. No one, not even someone claiming great spiritual power, not even someone in your own head, has the right to undermine your writing ambitions.

Your Bone Pointer stamps his foot and puffs out his chest. His t-shirt reads *I ♥ Cursing People*. Really, Bone Pointer? Really? He grabs the nearest object, mutters some mumbo jumbo over it, aims it in your direction.

"Put down the remote." You shake your head, confounded by how you ever could have let someone so ridiculous fill you with fear. The doctors on TV are talking about the need for manic moms to have something they refer to as "adult time."

"It's time for you to leave," you say, shutting off the television and directing your Bone Pointer to the door.

"You haven't seen the last of me," your Bone Pointer blusters, scuffling away in his bald booties.

Sad but true, you think. But at least for now, the image of those flying feathers can't help but make you smile as you head to your desk to complete the work you have started.

The Great American Thing

A man walks into a writing workshop, waving the Stars and Stripes. An eagle holding a scroll in its beak inscribed with the words *E pluribus unum* is perched on his shoulder.

"What can I do for you?" the instructor asks, struck by such a display of patriotism.

"Name's Uncle Sam," the man says. "I want to write the Great American Novel!"

"Well, you can't write the Great American Novel," the instructor tells him.

"Why not?" The man opens his laptop. His screen saver shows an image of the Statue of Liberty.

"Because," the instructor says, "you don't have the right constitution."

Well, *I* think it's funny.

Anyway, I made up that joke for a reason. On a regular basis, a new writing client or workshop participant will say the same thing to me, that his goal is to write the Great American Novel. Come to think of it, this person has always been a man, which makes me wonder if this is a random peculiarity, or a gender thing. Do male writers tend to think in more grandiose terms? Do women tend to assume that writing the Great American Novel is too ambitious or braggy? Studies show that girls in our culture continue to be raised with more of an emphasis on politeness, while boys are taught from a young age that crying is for sissies. Do cultural influences and gender stereotypes such as these play out in the writing realm as well?

MAN: "I want to write the Great American Novel."

GENDER POLICE: "You're damn right you do, unless you're one of those bawl babies whose mommy only lets them write short fiction."

WOMAN: "I want to write the Great American Novel."

GENDER POLICE: "Well, doll, why don't you just marry yourself then, because no man's gonna put up with that kind of attitude."

My goodness, writers already have enough issues with the Should Police patrolling their thoughts—*You should go apple picking with your family instead of working on that scene you've been trying to finish for a month . . . You should write like David Foster Wallace, or Zora Neale Hurston, or the person whose story everyone gushed over in your MFA program . . . You should wait until everyone you ever knew is dead before writing your memoir . . .* And now, to think that we also have to contend with the Gender Police. No wonder authors invented pen names.

As a writing instructor, I like to think I am gender indifferent. If a man came up to me and said, "I want to write the Great American Novel!" I would tell him that he cannot, even if he looks just like that character from my joke. I would say this before reading a word he had written, before I knew anything about him beyond his odd tendency to dress like a national symbol. If a woman came up to me and said, "I want to write the Great American Novel!" I would appreciate the change of pace, and I would ask her where she got her boots if they are calf-length with a three-inch stacked heel, and come in dove gray, but in response to her authorial aspirations, I would tell her the same thing I told that Uncle Sam fellow: "Forget about it."

For that matter, I would offer the same seemingly negative response to any writer boldly embarking on a creative project, regardless of size or scope.

You cannot write a novel.

You cannot write a memoir.

You cannot write a short story, or an essay, or, for that matter, a smoke-long story, which, as the name implies, is intended to be read in about seven minutes, the average amount of time it takes to smoke one cigarette (which, interestingly enough, equates to the same amount of time that cigarette shortens your life).

I say this because these ambitions—novels, memoirs, essays— until they actually exist, are abstractions. Your unwritten novel is not a thing; it is a big, vague, unwieldy *whatever*. So approaching your creative project with the mindset *I'm going to write a novel!* can exhaust your psyche just as surely as if you were mentally dragging a piano to your writing desk.

As writers, as people, we do not have the mental constitution to deal in abstractions, at least not for long. We may set out determined to write a book about, say, childhood, or the evils of war, or overcoming grief, but very quickly our big ideas overwhelm us. How do we capture childhood in a memoir? What do we put in our novel to recreate the emotional impact of war or grief? For that matter, what exactly does it mean to write a novel? It may have seemed like a perfectly reasonable goal at first, to write a book, but that was before you actually sat down to write it, at which point all your mind could conjure up was something looming and amorphous. With lots of words. So, so, so many words.

And do not think the conceptual weight of an essay or even flash fiction is any lighter. It's like that brainteaser: What weighs more, a ton of bricks or a ton of feathers? Even if the genre in which you intend to write is defined, in part, by its brevity, the idea or theme that your story embodies is still likely to be substantive enough to make your knees buckle, especially if you carry it around with you for too long a period.

Now imagine if your aspiration is to write the Great American Novel, making an impossible task, if possible, even more impossible, because the Great American Novel piles abstractions on top of abstractions. I mean, what is such a thing? One source defines the Great American Novel as a work of fiction that captures the culture of the United States at a specific time, and the unique perspective and experience of the common American citizen. This, I cannot get my head around. What defines the common American citizen? I don't even have much in common with my closest neighbors with whom I share a condo wall, at least based on what I have glimpsed in their recycling bin. Other definitions of this concept suggest that it is a benchmark of American literature in a given time period, and, theoretically, the greatest American book ever written.

There you have it. The greatest American book ever written. Have fun dragging that idea to your writing table before you sit down to work.

Thank goodness for William Carlos Williams, a literary force published in the first half of the twentieth century, and the man I credit for saving aspiring authors from the overwhelm of abstraction. Williams captured his poetic method in this opening line from his work "Paterson," which reads, "No ideas but in things." Though Williams left the phrase open to interpretation, it is generally understood that what he meant was for poetry to deal in real stuff, concrete objects like a red wheelbarrow, or snakes, or a blizzard, rather than dwell in the language of abstractions: truth, love, loss. Grounded in this concrete imagery, the writing evokes the abstraction on a more visceral level, making the idea all the more tangible and powerful. This is comparable to the goal of the popular maxim for storytelling: *Show don't tell.* In other words, don't just write down that your character is mad or sad or antsy; reveal the emotion through scenic elements.

Consider the following compare and contrast:

Telling: *Alicia loathed her husband.* Okay, so we get the concept that Alicia is not fond of her hubby, but do we really get it, not just on a head level, but on a bone-marrow level?

Showing: *"It's for my husband's birthday." Alicia handed the clerk the* XXL *lime-green sweater vest she'd pulled from the clearance rack. Don wore a size medium and preferred neutral colors. He was a bank president, after all, and didn't everyone know it. "Do you have gift wrapping?" she asked, digging through her Hermes bag for her wallet. "Preferably something in an even brighter shade of green."* Here is the idea—the abstraction of "loathing"—concretized through those all-important tangibles: significant details, action, thoughts, dialogue. This is the stuff that makes up a scene. These are the *things* that make abstractions and feelings accessible to the reader. Equally important, these are the things that make the task of writing accessible to you, the person who has to make it all happen.

"No ideas but in things." I love the simplicity and directness of this guidance. From what I have read, Williams, like his work, had a straightforward and unpretentious nature, in contrast to some of his more lofty modernist peers. Maybe because he worked full time as a family doctor and pediatrician, stealing moments to write poetry on prescription pads, and probably walking around with baby spit-up on his lapels, he understood that the stuff of everyday life was the stuff that mattered. How fitting, then, that a man who went to work every morning as a doctor would articulate one of the most useful bits of advice for writing well, and for a writer's well-being.

For writers to actually transmogrify abstract concepts into powerful prose, first we must bring them down to earth. We need to stop thinking in terms of writing a novel, and instead focus on writing about some thing, some object or concrete specific related to said novel. Consider these two different mindsets: *Oh God, I have to work on my novel* versus *Oh boy, my protagonist just bought herself roller derby skates.*

Roller derby skates are a thing. You can write about roller derby skates, using them to stir your creative juices. With roller derby skates you have your *in*, a way to launch a scene that can grow through those "showing" elements that I referred to earlier: significant details, action, thoughts (aka internal monologue), and likely some salty dialogue, all of which, when mingled together in the right proportions, will enable you to show your story. An example:

> First jam of the bout. The ref held her whistle, waiting for some screw-up with the clock to be fixed. Mitz glanced down at her hot pink skates, the laces triple-knotted. The pack was lined up on the track, the air already heavy with the smell of sweat and Lorna's perfume. "What did you roll in?" Mitz elbowed Lorna, and wrinkled her nose. Lorna gave Mitz the finger and grinned. Lorna was a helluva blocker, on the track and off, Mitz thought, so who cared if she doused herself in cheapo toilet water.

Writing about the roller derby is an accessible assignment, and, based on my first attempt in this particular storyscape, I can tell you it is also a lot of fun. And not once while working on that passage did I feel the burden of writing about an abstraction, for example, friendship. Yet look at how that concept ended up on the page.

No ideas but in things.

If roller derby skates do not figure into your story, then pick another object that does—an umbrella stand, a sword, a belt, sunflower pollen . . . Objects, we can get our minds around. Objects are the gifts we give ourselves as writers, real things we can describe and manipulate. Objects are what allow us to capture our ideas and make them manifest on the page. This is why I say, forget about writing a novel. Bury that abstraction deep in your mind, so deep that it cannot even reach the sublevels of your unconscious and cause you to have thinly disguised nightmares in which a piano with computer keys is chasing you down a hallway, and for some reason you are not wearing any clothes.

It is not my nature as a teacher or human being to discourage people from their ambitions; the world puts us in our place just fine on its own, and does not need any help from me. I also want to be clear that when I tell someone she cannot write the book or story she wants to write, this comment bears no reflection on her talent or abilities. I know that much of the culture of writing is intended to smoke out poseurs, to discourage people as a form of judgment or a test of their mettle. This is why some instructors take a boot-camp approach in their MFA classes or workshops— If you don't break under brutal attack of your work and personality, then maybe, just maybe, you have the guts to be a writer. My teaching philosophy is exactly the opposite. I believe that if people show up to a writing group, they are writers, assuming they choose to acquire the craft and practice the discipline required of the job. I also believe that each of us has a Great American Novel somewhere inside us, regardless of where we were born or reside. Who is to say that we don't? The challenge for all of us, however, is to materialize this sweeping goal into tangibles that we can actually write.

A few months ago, I went to a naturalization ceremony in my home state of Vermont. The ceremony took place in the gold-domed State House in Montpelier, and welcomed sixty-seven candidates from twenty-eight countries to American citizenship. The

Greek Revival building, with its marble floors, spiral staircases, and paintings of historic figures and battle scenes, befitted the occasion. This was, truly, a moving experience to witness, as people from far-flung countries—Bhutan, Poland, Somalia, Vietnam, Serbia, Germany, Canada, Costa Rica—collected on this point on the globe, and recited in unison the Oath of Allegiance . . . "That I will support and defend the Constitution and laws of the United States of America . . ."

I bring up this story because it underscores the point of this chapter. Just like the Great American Novel is an abstraction, so too is the idea of an American. What does it really mean to be a citizen of a nation that extends from sea to shining sea? How can a single concept embody millions and millions of people? How does one begin to translate the metaphor of a melting pot to reality?

No ideas but in things.

An American is George Washington in a powdered wig, whose gold-framed portrait graces the front of the grand assembly hall where the naturalization ceremony took place.

An American is the stooped, dark-skinned woman wrapped in a vibrant red robe and headscarf. She is steadied by her son's arm as she claims her US citizenship certificate from the presiding judge.

An American is each of the four Color Bearers from the American Legion, Post 3. They march in formation, bearing the national colors in white-gloved hands, their shiny silver helmets reflecting the light from the ornate chandelier.

An American is me, who loves this country because I can be who I want to be, including someone who abhors the United States' paucity of gun control, and celebrates the anniversary of women earning the right to vote and National Dog Day, which, oddly enough, both fall on the same date.

Our individuality, our past and present, our ideas, our ideals— they are all made manifest by the things we show, the things we

say and do and think, the things we carry. At times we, quite literally, wear our abstractions on our sleeves, or wrapped around our
heads in a brightly colored scarf. Like the idea of an American,
the idea of a novel—your Great American Novel, or short story,
or memoir, or essay—can be made manifest in the same way. A
focus on things in your prose or poetry not only will make your
writing ambitions doable, but this mindset will ultimately bring
forth in the most powerful way those ideas that you want to capture; those ideals that matter the most to you.

So, with that in mind, let's try this again, my second attempt
at joke writing.

> A man, no, a woman, walks into a writing workshop,
> waving the Stars and Stripes. An eagle holding a scroll in its
> beak inscribed with the words *E pluribus unum* is perched on
> her shoulder.
>
> "What can I do for you?" the instructor asks. By now she
> is used to such displays of patriotism, and can anticipate why
> this writer has come to her.
>
> "Name's Mitz," the woman says. "I want to write the Great
> American Novel!"
>
> "Terrific," the instructor says, excited at the prospect of
> helping another aspiring author achieve her dreams. "Then
> grab your hot pink skates because we're heading to the
> roller derby."

> *Forget all rules, forget all restrictions, as to taste,*
> *as to what ought to be said, write for the pleasure of it.*
> WILLIAM CARLOS WILLIAMS

Close your eyes. Imagine a character (or yourself) in a specific room. Look around. When your attention lands on a particular object, write about it. Where is the object located in the room? How do you or your character interact with it? What is its backstory or significance? The object is your *thing*; now expand your description into a scene by adding further detail, action, internal monologue, or pithy dialogue. Watch how an idea emerges as the scene develops.

Every. Single. Day.

Much to my surprise, my first "real" job out of college was not as a writer for a celebrity magazine, which had been my career goal as a dual major in journalism and English. Instead, I found myself working as a receptionist-slash-debt collector at one of those strip-mall finance companies that approve anyone for a loan as long as they agree to extortion in the form of grossly inflated interest rates. Note when I say "anyone," I am talking about honest, hardworking Americans, deadbeats, and me.

At the time, I was living in the fourth bedroom of my parents' house, overly dependent on the family dog, Olive, for company. Olive was a neurotic, graying mutt who tried to manage her anxiety by standing in an empty bathtub. I was just as anxious, at a complete loss as to how to kick-start a professional future from a beanbag chair in my childhood bedroom. For me, there was no comfort in an empty bathtub, so I took the first prospect of a paycheck from a job where I would not be serving beer. It was time, unfortunately, to enter the real world.

I hated everything about that job at the finance company. Anemic streaks of sunlight from the wrong-facing windows striated the generic decor. Putty-colored filing cabinets dominated one wall. Each file contained a double-sided loan application, mostly requesting money for utilitarian things like appliances or used cars. To see adulthood reduced to a stacked washer/dryer gave me a glimpse of a future that both depressed and scared me.

As a payment processor, I sat at a desk near the front entrance, where my job was to greet the debtors and record their weekly payments. I also took new applications, which included calculating for the customers the total cost of the loan after interest, for which I always felt compelled to apologize. My boss, Deanna, had an office behind me where she could hear everything I said, and then use it against me to point out my failings as a loan shark. Picture Deanna this way: a busty grenade, with a management style that alternated between snapping orders and over-sharing trivia about her namesake, the popular 1940s singer and actor Deanna Durbin.

Our customers came from diverse ethnic backgrounds, the majority of them from the city, rather than the mostly white suburbs where I was raised. I like to think I am a people person, and even when I am not, I'm a nervous talker, but in that job I cannot recall ever feeling comfortable enough to attempt banter or an actual conversation. What if in my youthful naïveté and eagerness to show that I was not a racist or classist, I inadvertently said something racist or classist? My own bank account could not afford appliances any more than those of our loan customers, yet I knew the security of my parents' fourth bedroom had colored my world, an expression that perfectly exemplified why I was terrified to make small talk.

"Have you called the Suggs?" This would be Deanna, hovering by my shoulder, calling me out on my most dreaded responsibility, chasing down clients who were late with their weekly payments. "Tell them they need to come into the office today or we're calling the collection agency!"

Most of the deadbeats I had to pursue did not pick up the phone, or they told me bald-faced lies, or yelled at me for bothering them, and for their life's circumstances. This was unpleasant, but not nearly as bad as calling the Suggs, who were not deadbeats. Just the opposite, in fact. The Suggs, much to my dismay, always took my calls, and made payments in person as soon as they had the money. Mr. Suggs's grim face had the pallor of a coffin lining, probably from working eighty hours a week at two jobs. When Mrs. Suggs hand-delivered a payment, she brought along their three kids, each one somber and obedient. Their little faces haunted me, as the family's account grew in arrears and Deanna insisted I keep harassing them.

"Have you called the Suggs?"

"Have you called the Suggs?"

"You know Deanna Durbin was almost cast as Dorothy in the Wizard of Oz."

"Have you called the Suggs?"

"Have you called the Suggs?"

Deanna—my boss, not the actor—was as relentless about deadbeats as she was about tugging down the blazer of the pant-suits she favored, which always seemed to instantly gap back open. "You keep at it," she demanded of me. "Every. Single. Day."

As writers, how many times have we heard a Deanna type preach to us about the need for vigilance in our work? How many times have we been on our own cases—*I should write every day! Joyce Carol Oates writes every day, eight hours a day. If I wrote every day, I could be Joyce Carol Oates!*

Now let's get real. Most of us are not Joyce Carol Oates. We do not have eight hours a day to write. We have legitimate excuses for not writing: our day jobs; our family obligations; a need for sleep.

Now let's get even more real. Sometimes we do not write for another reason that is harder to excuse, and that is that we just don't feel like it. Or at least I don't feel like it. There! I have said it. Sometimes, even if I have the time, even if my family and friends would love to get rid of me for a few hours, I just don't feel like writing! Does this make me an impostor? Does it make me seem ungrateful for the life of an artist? I am going to answer no because I am aware of lots of famous and not-famous writers who claim they also need to force themselves to write, and I would not judge them in this way. How it can be so hard to make ourselves do something we value so highly is one of those incongruities of human nature that defies explanation. But one thing I do know is that wanting to write, but not wanting to write, can lead to a lot of guilt.

We feel guilty for resolving to write every single day, and then not following through. We feel guilty for setting a lofty goal (*This is the year I will finish my book!*) and failing to meet that expectation. Sometimes, we even feel guilty when we are making great progress (*What kind of parent prefers to spend hours immersed in a dystopia of her own making, rather than help her kid with his algebra homework?*) And to top it all off, we feel guilty for feeling guilty because, really, what is the point? Guilt rarely inspires us to write, and only sours the experience of not writing.

To distract ourselves from all this guilt requires a special kind of mental gymnastics. That is why we assign urgency to tasks like depilling our sweaters, or organizing our light bulbs in order of wattage. Such tasks require little brain energy but induce a feeling of accomplishment. We also try to trick ourselves into thinking we are writing, when in fact what we are actually doing is *procrasti-writing*, for example, composing clever Facebook commentaries that are often more inspired than the first drafts we create of our stories. We may even try to shift the blame for not writing onto other people. *I was all set to work on my novel when Sybil called and made me go out with her for happy hour.*

Sometimes, all this guilt becomes too much to bear and we feel compelled to confess. "I haven't been writing!" This is how I am greeted on a regular basis by my author friends, or by former workshop participants I encounter around town. No "Hello." No "My goodness, you look absolutely stunning this morning!" Just an unsolicited admission of their crime. When this happens, I am tempted to respond, "What am I, the writing police?" but of course I am in a way, at least to the people in my classes who count on my deadlines and the accountability that a workshop provides.

Here is another typical exchange among guilt-logged writers:

"How was your writing day?"

Heavy sigh. "Not good. I didn't get nearly as much done as I had wanted."

Way back when, I might have taken the heavy sigher at her word, but not anymore. Not after hearing too many writers bemoan their lack of productivity, only to find out that they had indeed made progress, accumulating words, paragraphs, scenes, or pages that they had simply discounted as *not enough*. In fact, I have caught myself engaging in this same warped way of thinking.

"How's your manuscript coming along?" someone asks me.

"It's not," I say, feeling overwhelmed by all the words not written, all the challenges that lie ahead, and my recurring fear that I will die before the book is finished and people will think my first drafts are how I actually write.

Then time passes, and somehow my book is written. *Where the heck did those chapters come from?* I am truly befuddled by my progress. But of course my book, like all those other books authored by heavy sighers, got written while I was so distracted by guilt over my lack of progress that I did not see what was happening when I was right there in the room.

Writers need a bar. I do not mean the kind of bar typically associated with authors, though the thought does bring to mind a wonderful image. On one stool at the far end of the counter perches the aforementioned Joyce Carol Oates, nursing her eight-hours-a-day writing habit, surrounded by 100 or so of her published books. At the other end of the bar sits Grace Paley, who was often asked during interviews why she had written so little—three story collections and three chapbooks of poetry in seventy years. Paley offered a variety of answers to this question, the most notable being this response: "Art is too long, and life is too short." The image of these two distinguished authors, comfortably ensconced at opposite ends of the long, polished counter, suggests great longitude in what defines a worthy amount of output.

When I say writers need a bar, however, what I mean is a tangible measure of productivity tailored to each of our creative processes and temperaments. Your bar may be higher or lower than my bar, but the same rules would apply. If your productivity falls below the level of achievement you have set for yourself, then, and only then, can you feel guilty about your slacker tendencies. Otherwise, give yourself a break. In my opinion, just having such a bar would help relieve us of the burden of free-floating guilt, while also establishing a degree of discipline in our creative lives.

Of course, I have borrowed this concept from a variety of successful writers, whose own bars take the form of daily word counts. For example, Graham Greene claimed that he committed to 500 words a day for five days a week, and when he reached that amount, he stopped working, even if he was in the middle of a scene. Historian Shelby Foote wrote his massive three-volume account of the Civil War at about the same 500-words-a-day pace. Margaret Meade established a habit of getting up at five o'clock every morning to write 1,000 words before breakfast. At the higher end of the bar, both Arthur Conan Doyle and Anne Rice listed 3,000 words as their daily quota. Ernest Hemingway did not subscribe to a daily word count, but set a goal of "one true sentence" to get started, and advised novelists to always stop for the day when they knew what was going to happen next. That way they would never be stuck.

The value of breaking down any task into small increments is well supported by the science of motivation. Researchers in this field have determined that having "macro goals," or dreaming big, is only part of the secret to success. It is not enough to visualize the lofty goal—a finished book! You also need to envision the process and establish "micro quotas" for consistent progress. To help with this, researchers recommend creating an accountability chart, on which you note what you did, and when you did it. The beauty of such a chart is that it shows you in black and white your process for making progress. Or not.

Because willpower is a limited resource, it also behooves us not to rely on it too heavily to do anything. One way to reduce the need for willpower is to create shortcuts, literally, between ourselves and our work. This translates to simply having the computer open or the notepad nearby, so you can just plunk down and get started—no extra motivation needed to find your way to another room. In addition, because our brains like contingency plans, there is a useful technique called "if-then planning," for when you are *this close* to caving. An example of an if-then plan might be something like this: "If I am feeling insecure about my abilities, then I will read a few pages of my favorite past work to motivate me." Another planning technique that helps reduce the distraction of too many choices is to decide your priority tasks the night before, rather than waiting until morning: *Tomorrow, I will get up and start right in killing off that pesky neighbor character!*

Productivity experts also insist that we eliminate the temptation to multitask, for example by being online when we are writing. When researchers studied the work patterns of multitaskers and analyzed their ability to (1) filter information, (2) switch between tasks, and (3) maintain a high working memory, they found that multitaskers were terrible at all three. In other words, multitaskers are bad at every aspect of multitasking, even though they have the illusion that they are being more productive.*

*I remain unconvinced that multitasking is impossible or always counterproductive. As a student, I had no trouble whispering in class while following the lecture. "Joni! What did I just say?" teachers would demand. Despite my divided attention, I always could repeat their words. Now, as a writer, I think my creativity is often served by bouncing between projects within the same work session, or filling in lulls with Internet searches for, say, the world's cutest animals, which tends to stimulate my thinking, refresh my editorial lens, and make me wish I had an African pygmy hedgehog.

And finally, beware of the "what-the-hell effect," where one slipup becomes an excuse to abandon all self-control. This effect is most commonly associated with dieters, but it also applies to writers, and especially writers on diets. We tell ourselves we are going to write every day, no exceptions, but then when the inevitable happens and we miss a day, we figure we might as well take off the rest of the week. Or month. Or year. *What the hell*, we think as we shove potato chips into our mouths. Once we fall out of the habit of writing, it can be a long and high-caloric road back.

Macro goals. Micro quotas. Accountability charts. Contingency plans. As writers, we may dwell in the arts, but thank goodness for the science of motivation. I can personally vouch for all of these productivity techniques because I have tried them all, failed at them all, and then tried them all again because I know, without them, I would have fewer words to my credit, and even more guilt about not always wanting to write. Still, if I think too much about all these things we are told to do day after day to keep deadbeat writers like myself on track, it can get to be too much. In fact, it can trigger unpleasant memories of a relentless voice from my past, accompanied by a tug on a blazer.

"Have you called the Suggs?"

"Have you called the Suggs?"

"In 1938, Deanna Durbin won a Juvenile Academy Award."

"Have you called the Suggs?"

"Have you called the Suggs?"

If my experience at the strip-mall finance company taught me anything, it was that relentlessness for the sake of relentlessness is a poor use of time and energy. Not once did my daily habit of harassing the Suggs extract a faster payment. They were tapped out, and so was I. We all need time to refill our coffers.

And so I would like to end this chapter not with thoughts of Deanna, my unexploded grenade of a boss, or the downtrodden

Suggs, who did indeed pay off their debt in full as soon as they had the money, or even the popular singer and actor Deanna Durbin, whose real first name, ironically, was not Deanna but Edna Mae. Rather, I will close with an instructional story intended to address what is probably the hardest part of doing anything on any given day, and that is just getting started.

Once upon a time my friend Alison was an acrobatic pilot who wanted to build her own plane. So she ordered a kit for a RANS S-10, a small, aerobatic aircraft made of steel and aluminum and fabric. One day, a tractor-trailer arrived at her house with a giant crate filled with all kinds of tubing, cables, an engine, fuel tanks, tires, a propeller, bags full of nuts and bolts, and a thick assembly manual.

Alison worked nights and weekends on her plane, making slow progress. Still, so much remained to be done—wiring, instruments, control systems, wings! Would her aircraft ever leave the ground? Would she ever fulfill her dream of doing barrel rolls and hammerheads in a machine of her own making? Across the country sat thousands of half-completed planes covered by tarps, abandoned by owners who had felt overwhelmed, just like Alison was starting to feel now.

Like most people who attempt to make their own planes, Alison belonged to an organization called the Experimental Aircraft Association. After she had been working on her project for about a year, one of the organization's volunteer advisors paid her a visit. She shared with him that she was worried the job was too big, and that she was going to fail. Her advisor looked at all the parts of her unfinished plane scattered around her garage. More parts cluttered her basement.

"Don't think about all the things you have left to do," he said. "Just touch the airplane three times a week."

After that, Alison no longer felt so overwhelmed. At least three days a week, she headed to her workbench, picked up some small component, ran her hand along a piece of tubing or cable. An hour or two would pass, and the next thing she knew, more parts were fastened together, another rib was riveted, a pedal was bolted to the cockpit floor.

Just touch the airplane. I think there is something so compelling, so right about this gentle advice. That was all the motivation Alison needed to finish building her plane a few years after that huge crate arrived in her driveway. When I am feeling particularly resistant to quotas and accountability, I call on those words to beckon me to my own workbench, with the only expectation to visit the page, to get a feel for my story. Who knows? Maybe some ideas or scenes will fit together. And maybe, I hope, the next time you find yourself reluctant to approach your writing, or feel overwhelmed by the size of your dreams, this advice—this invitation—will prove just what you need to help you fly.

The Church of the Creative Process

"How do you know God exists if you can't see Him?"

Whenever I hear someone ask that question, my first thought is, *Him? What is this, 1958?* Then my second thought is this: Oh no, not another one of those "New Atheists." These are a rising tide of modern thinkers who do not just eschew religion, but hope to incite a religion apocalypse, with only scientific theory, empirical evidence, and an atomic whirl rising from the ashes. Whereas the "Old Atheists" were more inclined to allow for the coexistence of religion and science as complementary ways of making sense of the world, the New Atheists show an intolerance of any kind of religious faith. One prominent voice in the movement wrote that anybody who doesn't believe in evolution must be stupid, insane, or ignorant. Another fellow, an evolutionary biologist and best-selling author, espouses that science is the only way to discover what is real. He argues that while religion is about believing what we would like to believe, even when there is no evidence or way to adjudicate that faith, science contains powerful accepted knowledge. You cannot believe one thing when science proves another, he insists. Therefore, science and faith are mutually exclusive.

On good days, I would consider myself a spiritual person, but I am not at all religious and have never belonged to a church. The first time I encountered Jesus was when I was about eight years old, and read an illustrated children's book of Bible songs at the dentist's office. Growing up in Lancaster, Pennsylvania, where one of the first questions people asked was what church you attended, it was a relief to finally have some talking points of my own: "Yes, Jesus loves me. This I know, for the Bible tells me so." Now as an adult, the only time I regret my lack of formal religion is when I think about dying or going to prison, but my hope is that I'll be one of those people who conveniently converts during a crisis.

On a related note, while I don't like the idea of ape ancestors, I do believe in natural selection, and I cannot believe that certain boards of education in the United States of America still argue that intelligent design and other creationist ideas be taught as viable alternatives to evolution in science classrooms. I understand why the New Atheists get so testy in a world where religious dogma is used to promote destructive agendas, from terrorism, to denying global warming, to discouraging childhood vaccinations.

In short, I am inclined to sit on the same side of the room as the New Atheists, though I suspect my humor would be lost on them. Regardless, I still take exception to their stance that the only reality is that which is proven by science. Yes, empiricism should always trump willful idiocy, but to suggest that we can believe only in that which is determined by evidence-based knowledge is to overlook the fact that science cannot account for all the things we do not know or cannot know; all the things that are yet to be discovered but do exist, or will exist, if we just have a little faith.

In the writing world, I am here to tell you brothers and sisters that science and faith are not mutually exclusive. In fact, we must submit to both, and call upon both at the same time, if we are to meet our writing goals and be happy in our creative lives.

As people who want our written words to communicate and mean something to others, we cannot deny the evidence. The science of creative writing—also known as narrative craft—has certain realities. What follows are just three examples of what we know to be true because they have been proven since the origin of stories.

1 *Showing is better than telling.* This specifically holds true
  when it comes to recreating the emotional impact of
  experience. Irrefutable evidence for this exists in the works
  of both cave and contemporary writers who create scenes
  so vivid you find yourself tearing up over the death of
  some long-dead or fictitious antelope. That is the power of
  showing.

2 *Backstory usually makes for a lousy opening.* As much as you
  may feel your readers need to know about your narrator's
  childhood and psychological history before the actual
  story kicks in, they do not. A lot of setup or exposition or
  description, even if it is well written, makes readers antsy
  for the "now" of the story, otherwise knows as the "present
  tense of the narrative." Readers like to be grounded in
  time and place and situation from early on. They want to
  be immersed in the actual story (read plot) before you lay
  a lot of information on them. *Why is the author telling me
  all this stuff?* they wonder, and not in a good way, because
  until the actual story begins, the backstory is not really
  relevant. And if you keep readers waiting too long for the
  "now" of the story, they are going to get peevish and likely
  stop reading. Editors provide proof of this type of natural
  selection when they turn down a manuscript after reading
  only a few pages, citing in the rejection letter, "If you can't
  hook me on page one . . ."

3 *Main characters must act rather than just be acted upon.*
  To be a worthy protagonist or narrator, a main character
  must want something and act on that desire. This can
  take the form of external action—uncovering clues, car
  chases, confrontations. Equally compelling is the action
  of the mind. In many a powerful work, this internal
  action, and the resulting shift in your central character's
  mental landscape, is where the real drama lies. It can be

confusing when readers discount a book, saying, "Nothing happened," and yet the pages are filled with action scenes. What is causing that reaction, however, is that nothing seemed to have happened inside your main character's head; his or her mental landscape did not seem to be affected by the events of the story.

These three examples of proven narrative techniques offer hard evidence that if we want to achieve powerful prose, we must adhere to the science of creative writing. Narrative craft is what gives life to our stories, whether those stories are real or fictional. But here is another reality, less tangible but no less irrefutable. Faith is what gives life to craft.

To state the obvious—writing can be challenging. Not to be blasphemous, but if you think turning water into wine is some trick, try capturing love, or parenthood, or grief on the page. Try turning a rambling collection of half-baked ideas and sloppy sentences with mismatched tenses into polished prose. Even seasoned writers struggle during the dark days of the drafting process. In fact, seasoned writers sometimes struggle even more than newbies because of their heightened awareness of craft. When we are so keenly aware of the need to create complex characters; the need to sustain profluence; and the need for about a bazillion other techniques to achieve what we want to achieve on the page, we may be even more prone to despair. It can feel so overwhelming at times, this awareness of what *isn't* there. How can you trust that your roiling swirl of disjointed scenes could possibly be the origin of anything sustainable? For that matter, where is the proof of yourself as Creator, when the fruits of your labor reveal serious weaknesses in the form of a slow start, or a saggy middle, or a main character too passive to even lift a finger to save your sorry drafts?

But it is in the throes of those sorry drafts that faith plays the most critical role. These are the times when we need to just put down whatever words lurch from our fingertips. We need to stop questioning and second-guessing. We need to believe that whatever writing we manage in the moment is part of a bigger plan. This is what it means to have faith in the creative process. Yes, adhere to the science of writing, practice craft, draft your way forward by employing proven narrative techniques, but also trust in the invisible, higher power of the process.

The New Atheists laud the hegemony of doubt. They caution: "Don't fool yourself into believing something just because you want to believe it." As writers, however, we cannot let doubt dominate our efforts. When we do not believe what we want to believe —that we can and will create the works we want to create—then no craft can save us. Without faith in the creative process, we are too likely to stray from our notepads or laptops and find ourselves not on the path to clarity, but leaning against some concrete pillar in an underground parking lot, sneaking an e-cigarette that tastes like kiwi.

I am one to talk. Maybe it's because the extent of my formal religious training came from a dentist's office, but when I am working on any given draft, I experience a lot of crises of faith. And by a lot, I mean that in almost every writing session, there comes a moment when I feel hopeless, exhausted, and ravenous all at once. *What the hell am I trying to say?* This is my standard cry into the wilderness during my worst moments of doubt. Because of the frequency of these crises, I have (almost) accepted the reality that they are a normal, even a purposeful part of the process. Normal or not, it can be hard not to get up, or give up, during these difficult times. At its foundation, the act of writing is a spiritual practice, in that it should feed our spirit, and not merely be a means to an end. When we experience doubt, how can we evangelize ourselves as artists? Where can we turn to renew our own faith?

Several years ago, I returned to my hometown for a visit only to discover that a group of zealous believers had erected the biggest church I have ever seen, only a mile or so from the house where I grew up. Now this was something! But what? The church—actually it resembles more of a compound for a suburban dictator—sprawls across acres of land. It dwarfs the nearby farm museum and cemetery. When services let out, traffic is tied up forever on Butter Road as onward go the Christian soldiers, home to their ball games and backyard barbecues, and the other graces that constitute our middle-class lives. No matter how many times I drive by that church when I am back in Lancaster, it makes me feel uneasy. In fact, it makes me feel the opposite of spiritual. Why the need for such a fortress of faith? If I were one of those New Atheists, I might see these types of mega-churches—replete with stages rather than alters, lobby cafes, and even bowling alleys in the basement—as proof indeed, not of God, but of our human tendencies toward overcompensation.

In life, bricks and mortar can make a powerful statement, but it seems to me that a single cell, and its ability to divide and replicate and renew itself, is more than enough to engender faith in something wondrous beyond our immediate scope of understanding. In writing, embedded within the creative process is a parallel type of cell cycle. Within the smallest structural unit of a nascent story or poem exists the possibility of it growing into a mature work. When I am full of doubt, it helps to return my focus to a molecular level. If I can find a single word that is just the right word, that is a sign. If I can achieve one effective scene, then why not assume I can replicate that effort? Word by word, scene by scene; the creative process sees me through the wilderness of those early drafts.

As a writing teacher, how can I not have faith in the creative process when I have witnessed what comes of it? Here I am not talking about my own experience, but that of other writers who have shared with me their own doubts, their own drafts. Thanks to them, I have witnessed life breathed into once flat characters. I have seen form emerge from chaos. I have seen graceless wording transformed into inspired prose. This is what happens when believers trust in the creative process. And when I say believers, I am not talking about a chosen few. I am talking about all those people in my groups, and at writing conferences around the country, and laboring alone at home at their desks in their slightly damp-smelling basements, who keep at it even when they feel discouraged and clueless. There is an expression—blind faith—that the New Atheists probably love because it makes something they already pooh-pooh—faith—seem even more ridiculous by tagging on a needless modifier. But the reality is that you will be writing blind a good part of the time; and in fact, writing without understanding or discrimination actually serves the creative process in important ways. You need to trust that there are parts of the creative process you cannot see, parts that work in mysterious ways, guided by whatever you want to call it—your unconscious, your muse, your higher power. You need to remember this because, with faith, you will find a way to do the work necessary to manufacture meaning out of material. Without faith, another unfinished project is likely to end up in the abyss of your bottom drawer.

Craft is corporeal. It is as tangible as an active verb. It is as constructed as a scene, and as knowable as the rules of grammar. With craft, you can skillfully manipulate and remanipulate words on a page, and that cognitive undertaking is a beautiful thing. But craft made manifest through faith—a faith in the creative process, a faith in yourself—now, that is the stuff of inspiration.

Like any creative effort, be it the evolution of a species or the development of a work of literary merit, we are informed by inarguable truths. Through the tools of science and narrative techniques, we can understand the parts that go into creation. Through time and drafts, we are able to follow the trajectory that leads to the sum of those parts. But what we cannot know, what cannot be proven is something equally real, but only attainable through faith, and that is the divine mystery that allows the whole to become *greater* than the sum of those parts. That is the miracle of life. That is the miracle of the creative process. And when you believe in miracles, anything is possible.

SEEING
BLUE

The suffering artist's spouse.

Drama Queen

For someone who is always telling her writing students to create scenes, it's ironic how averse I am to them in real life. I do not like *Sturm und Drang*, neither the air-stopping glottalization it requires to say the expression, nor the concept of extreme emotionalism. If people make a scene in public, say, yelling at the cashier at Walgreen's because she won't take their expired coupons, I feel compelled to watch, of course, but it has the same disturbing aftereffects as eating a Whoopie Pie. Once the rush has passed, I am left feeling cheap, ashamed, and disinclined to look at my teeth in the mirror. As for other displays of emotion, crying for example, I understand that tears befit certain situations, such as when an author reads an authentically moving piece, or if the situation has anything to do with dog rescues; but weeping, weeping is like crying into a microphone. (Are you really that sad, or maybe one little part of you likes the attention?) On a related note, I am also suspicious of dramatic affectations, including but not limited to the slo-mo replay, addressing fellow workshop participants as "Darling," and capes.

To my knowledge, my mother never used the word "darling" or owned a cape. Regardless, I am certain that my dislike of high drama is directly tethered to her. This is not, I repeat, *not* because I buy into the myth that mothers are always to blame when a child has issues or exhibits aberrant behavior. I believe I speak for all mothers when I say that if our grown-up, or almost grown-up daughters make bad decisions, for example choosing to attend a college hundreds of miles away from home, this has nothing to do with our parenting qualities or coaster policies. (Really? There's a coaster on the table two centimeters from where you're sitting, and you still can't manage to land your sweaty glass on it?)

Still, when it comes to my disdain for high drama, I think it is fair to say that my own mother played a significant role, thanks in particular to one defining incident in a parental career character- ized by fierce love, with equal interludes of hollering and smiting, when she was in one of her moods.

When I was a child, my mother threw a twenty-eight-pound tur- key across our kitchen. Right in front of me. This was on Thanks- giving Day, which might explain my antipathy toward gratitude lists. I cannot remember the exact year this turkey-throwing in- cident occurred, only that it had to be one of my most formative ones because the scene imprinted on my mind as irrevocably as the scorch marks left by the hot grease on the linoleum floor.

As context, I can tell you that my mother was mad. (Read mad as in angry, not insane, though in this particular case I would not put too fine a point on it.) My mother was even mad at me, the "baby" of the family, who rarely got caught doing anything wrong. We were in the kitchen. She was banging pans and muttering about how my lazy-ass older sisters and my father (watching the pregame show in the family room) could not be bothered to lift a finger. I was overcompensating for the rest of my family's failures by madly peeling potatoes. This was the backstory to my mother's foul mood. Later that afternoon, when the meat thermometer jabbed into the turkey's flank confirmed that she had missed her opportunity to food poison all of us, she summoned everyone to help carry the prepared feast into the dining room. For the record, I arrived swiftly, but, apparently, the others failed to respond in a manner in keeping with my mother's need for timeliness. Thus I, and I alone, witnessed the scene: my mother's monstrous oven mitts gripping the handles of the turkey-laden roasting pan, and awkwardly swinging it outward, as if emptying a full bucket of slop water. The bird soared briefly, belying the myth that turkeys can't fly, then landed with a juicy thud, skidded across the floor, and ricocheted off the metal grill on the bottom of the fridge. Remarkably, when the turkey came to rest in front of the sink, most of the bread stuffing remained intact in the bird's chest cavity.

"What the hell?" my dad said as he entered the kitchen. He looked down at the grease-splattered floor and belly-up bird. Then he looked at me, since my mother had already headed upstairs with a slapped-together plate of strawberry salad and olives. My birth order dictated that I function as the family entertainer, a service I often provided in the hope of offsetting tension between my parents, but this event was too much, even for me, a master at manufacturing desperate merriment. I grabbed a roll of paper towels and started slopping up the mess, my knees slipping on the slick linoleum. I remember resenting the fact that neither my dad nor my lazy-ass sisters helped me with the cleanup. I also remember thinking that Thanksgiving, second only to my birthday on my list of favorite holidays, had now been ruined forever for me, and for no reason at all.

Fast-forward, thank goodness. As it turns out, Thanksgiving was not ruined forever, and eventually returned to its second-favorite status on my holiday list. But that scene did set a course for a life where I have made a point to eschew anyone or anything even hinting at high emotionalism.

Or, so I thought.

Not too long ago, I was sitting at my writing desk in my bedroom. It had taken Herculean effort on my part to arrive in this chair by nine-ish, even though I had made a point to rise at 5 a.m., at great sacrifice to my health, given the importance of eight hours' sleep. In the kitchen, as I waited for my hazelnut-flavored coffee to brew, the containers of old leftovers in the back of the fridge screamed for my attention. Why couldn't my family finish meals? Why was Tupperware so demanding? By the time I had finished cleaning the fridge, and then tidying all our kitchen drawers, my anxiety about not writing dictated that I trawl the Internet for stress-reducing tips, which somehow led to my catching up on celebrity news, and ultimately posting more pictures of my cat on Facebook. Finally, after the cat refused to stay put for any more photographs, I was able to sequester myself in my bedroom workspace. By now, however, the rest of the members of the household were astir.

Le sigh.

I straightened a pile of papers on my desk. For confidence, I skimmed a book I had previously written that I still like, though as is often the case when I reread work from my past, I experienced a feeling of disassociation. *Who wrote that?* I thought, appreciating a passage. *That author was so lucky to have the words come out just as she had envisioned them in her head. I want to be an author!* I glared at my book jacket photo. Just look at her, smiling, with her hair all combed. *Authors have it so much easier than writers.* Resentment toward my former self darkened my mood further, even as the sane part of my mind was well aware that this previous book had not come any easier than the one I was wrestling with now.

A few minutes passed with little progress showing on my screen. The door to the bedroom opened.

"What?" I exploded.

"Socks. I just need a pair of socks." My boyfriend tiptoed across the carpet to our closet, each step a thunderous blow to my concentration.

My response was a tour de force of emotionalism expressed in both internal and external monologue.

Why does everyone always have to interrupt me?

No one understands how hard it is to write!

Couldn't people, just once, live without socks for a day?

I rose from my desk, then collapsed back into the chair.

I stared down my boyfriend until he left the bedroom, softly closing the door behind him. That's when I caught an image of myself in the full-length mirror on the back of the door. My shoulders cinched around my neck like a drawstring garbage bag, my face puckered like a loaf of punched-in sour dough. *Sturm und Drang.* Maybe because my barefoot boyfriend is German, or maybe because the person in the mirror brought to mind the title character in Wagner's eighteenth-century play *The Child Murderess,* those words popped into my head.

As writers, we have unhappy tendencies of which we may not always be aware. You would think that, given my post-traumatic turkey disorder, I would have been above this kind of high drama. In fact, I thought I was until that scene in the bedroom, when I realized something I had been blind to my entire writing life. I was a Drama Queen. Maybe not so much in my real life, but most certainly in my writing life. Here was my creative process: Procrastinate. Feel lousy about procrastinating. Take it out on everyone else. Eventually get to writing.

In the eighties, I used to watch the nighttime soap opera *Dynasty.* The show centered around the super-rich Carrington family, who resided in a palatial home in Denver and thrived on backstabbing, scandal, secret family alliances, and massacres! The show's main characters included the dashing, distant patriarch Blake Carrington, his scheming ex-wife Alexis, and his younger second wife Krystle, whose heart was as flawless as the blood diamond on her finger. In one scene, Krystle confronts Alexis about a horse-riding accident that took place in an earlier episode. She suspects Alexis was the mystery figure who fired the gun that caused her horse to buck, ending Krystle's pregnancy.

"You're jealous," Krystle accused Alexis, "jealous because I was going to give Blake a child and you couldn't stand that, could you?"

Alexis rejoined, "I didn't cause your accident, Krystle, just as I didn't cause your barrenness."

At the time, I remember thinking, *Who talks like that?* Then

I realized, I do. I blamed everything and everyone—from the kitchen drawers, to Netflix, to people who wear socks—for all the times my creative life felt barren. In *Dynasty*, the confrontation between Alexis and Krystle devolves into a scene in which the women awkwardly wrestle, knocking shoulder pads askew and revealing way too much pantyhose. Eventually, the grabbing and hair pulling give way to a pillow fight, and quickly feathers start to fly. The scene begs the question: Couldn't the Carringtons afford better-quality sofa accents? More to the point, isn't there a more effective, less mortifying way to resolve tension, creative and otherwise? Two decades later, that pillow-fight scene lives on, thanks to YouTube, and has become an iconic moment in television, the quintessential catfight between two hot women. This has to be a legacy of dubious distinction for the two elegant actors who played these characters.

As writers, we leave legacies of our own. Here, I do not mean the great works we have penned or will pen that we leave behind for future readers. Rather, I mean the *Sturm und Drang* that we manufacture in our writing lives. I know there are appropriate times to stir up a fuss. The world, even the people who love us most, do not always make it easy for us to write, and sometimes we have to throw fits, or pillows, or whatever it takes to claim our creative time. Still, if high drama is a pattern rather than a necessity, it begs the question—How is procrastinating, and then feeling angry at yourself for procrastinating, and then projecting that anger on the nearest breathing target, enabling your writing life or making you feel better?

"I didn't cause your accident, Krystle, just as I didn't cause your barrenness." In *Dynasty*, it turns out that Alexis was only half lying when she threw back her shoulder pads and recited that ridiculous dialogue. In fact, she was indeed the person who had fired the gun that caused Krystle's horse to buck on that fateful day. But Krystle was wrong in assigning Alexis blame for her barrenness, because, as it turns out, Krystle was not barren at all! She just needed to stop throwing pillows and get down to business, which is how she managed to deliver a beautiful baby girl three seasons later.

There is a lesson to be learned from all this, and it starts by recognizing that sometimes we cause more problems for ourselves than we might perceive, and the consequences of *Sturm und Drang* do not do our writing lives, or our relationships, any favors. With this in mind, it behooves us to try a little harder not to get worked up in our heads, and then outside our heads, whether we are procrastinating or finally sitting down at our desks. Why not conserve our emotional energy, and use our precious little writing time for more important things, like creating drama on the page?

Flying turkeys. Flying feathers. Temper tantrums over socks. Scenes like these may serve our stories, but in real life they have one thing in common: they make a mess. And then someone, likely you, with no help from anyone else, is left to clean them up, all the while wondering why some of the things to be most thankful for in life—like the gift of being a writer—has to be ruined for no reason at all.

Seeing Blue

I was heading to my Prius after leading one of my "Page Producers" workshops when someone called my name. A friend I had not seen for quite a while dashed across the street.

"What have you been up to?" she asked.

"I'm working on a book about creativity and happiness," I responded. "It looks at the ways we can work with, rather than against, our creative process to write more productively, and be less screwy." Usually I am more reserved when telling people who run up to me in the street about a work-in-progress, but I was in my own happy place. In the workshop that had just ended, our group had discussed the last chapter of a novel the writer had been drafting for years. In anticipation of this milestone, another participant had brought champagne to the meeting, which had warmed my heart.

"Have you read So-and-So's new book on creativity?" my friend interrupted my thoughts. "It's exactly like the book you're trying to write. I heard the author talking about it on NPR, and she sounds amazing!"

Whoosh. My happy place imploded. And don't think I am just talking metaphorically. My stomach clenched, like the time I hit that adorable chipmunk crossing the road. I don't believe my friend intended to make me feel physically sick and destroy my writing hopes and dreams with a single comment. She also didn't refer to this famous author as "So-and-So," but that is how I choose to refer to her in this chapter and for time immemorial, seeing as how "She Who Cannot Be Named" has already been taken.

"I'll bring you a copy of her book," my friend offered. "Maybe it will give you some good ideas."

"No thanks," I said. *I've just decided to quit writing forever and hide in my closet.* That last part was what I was thinking as we hugged goodbye.

There are so many reasons not to write. Take this very book you are now reading. Why would I think the world needed my thoughts on creativity and happiness, after being told that one of the world's most famous authors had recently covered the subject and already stolen all my potential NPR readers? Over the course of working on this manuscript, I really tried to forget about So-and-So. I knew that she only riled me up to no productive end— *That first best seller of hers was so contrived! And now she's gone and stolen my idea! And yes, it is fine to drink Vermouth during the day. Vermouth isn't even a real alcohol.* Because of thoughts like these, I went out of my way to try to purge So-and-So from my consciousness, avoiding, for example, the prominent display of new nonfiction releases in the front of every bookstore. This is an important responsibility we have as writers, to proactively avoid the books and situations that undermine our confidence, while seeking out those that inspire and teach us.

Unfortunately, however, the universe loves situational irony, and the more I tried to insulate myself from So-and-So, the more she dogged me. There I was, for example, minding my own business, trawling Designer Shoe Warehouse for online sales, when this author appeared in a pop-up ad promoting her podcast on creativity. Already, the creepy cyber-mentalists had uncovered my secret fear of intestinal worms, constantly blitzing me with unsolicited yet compelling infomercials. (*You'll never believe what's eating your insides!*) And now, equally invasive, a suggestion to "like" So-and-So right there next to my Facebook feed, plus links, links, and more links to her genius, infecting my computer like a Trojan virus!

I know there was a psychological factor in play, similar to when

you are thinking about buying a banana slicer, and then everywhere you go, someone is using a banana slicer. This cannot mean
a sudden run on banana slicers, but rather that you are noticing
them more. Still, more people kept insisting I read this author. I
met with a new writing client. Seated at the glass table in her elegant apartment, she asked me to read two pages, a sample of her
first attempt at writing personal narrative. Just two pages, and on
one she describes her time in a waiting room reading So-and-So's
book. Even my ex-husband, who supported my career as an author for over two decades of marriage by being a generous provider, while showing little interest in my creative work, suddenly
showed up after a trip with a page ripped from an airline magazine—a Q&A with So-and-So.

"I thought this might interest you," he said as he handed me
the article. "It sounds a lot like the book you're writing." I tried to
compose myself. My ex has served his time accommodating my
mental meltdowns. The page displayed more photo than type. So-
and-So is blue-eyed and blond like me, except her ends are free of
frizz. She is wearing a navy blue blouse, one of the only two colors
I can wear that don't sallow my complexion. A delicate gold watch
encircles her wrist. Basically, she is more polished, more authorial, more everything than me, which made it clear that she had
rendered me unnecessary not only as a writer, but as a person.

Here is a frightening truth. Every subject, every life experience,
every iteration of the seven basic plots, every theme related to life
and death and all the stuff in between has already been addressed
by writers who came before you, many of whom did a thorough
and bang-up job. Even the weirdo ideas out there have been covered across genres. My friend Dixie wrote a short story about a
talking stone. She read it at a flash fiction contest. One of the
judges opened his critique by saying, "If I hear one more talking
stone story . . ." In light of this judicial proclamation, where do we

go from here? How far do we have to reach to be original? Talking tanzanite? Talking moon rock? Logic dictates that in the 200,000 years modern humans have existed on this planet, we have exhausted the potential for new story ideas.

So why write? When you are on fire creatively, the question answers itself. But what about those times when you feel stuck, discouraged, ready to quit? When the writing comes hard, when somebody or something ambushes your confidence, what do you tell yourself? How do you not stop writing? These are the moments when our writing lives hang in the balance, so it behooves us to be clear about the reasons we do it, because, let's face it, there are plenty of good reasons to do something else.

When I was a freelance copywriter, companies used to hire me to create their taglines, those catchy phrases that differentiate a business and capture its essential appeal. At $1,500 a pop, writing taglines is, sadly, the most lucrative form of writing I will probably ever do, but do not assume that I didn't earn my paycheck. To come up with an effective slogan, you must identify both the rational and emotional benefits that drive people toward a decision. In addition, you need to understand which category of benefit matters more to your audience, and to what degree. I bring this up here because categorizing benefits also provides a useful way for you to gain an understanding of how much, and why, your writing matters to you.

I am in the business of selling writing, meaning that I want everyone to write because I know something of value always comes of it. If you were hesitating on the threshold of my classroom, I would insist you come on in, grab a lumpy chair, and then I would use your own writing to prove you belong there. In lieu of that, I will put on my copywriter's hat here, and meet you on your own threshold between coming and going. What follows are four benefits, rational to a one, to sell you on the fact that your writing matters.

1   *Your perspective.* Growing up in a hippie commune . . .
    traveling across Europe on a bicycle . . . losing a loved one
    to cancer. Yes, every type of experience has been covered,
    but you will always be the first one to do it through your
    lens. In creative nonfiction and fiction, it is not the subject
    matter that makes a work original, but how you react to it;
    how you render it on the page. This is why it's important
    to capture the story or personal experience through your
    distinct point of view, through specific details and an
    individualized synthesis of material and meaning. Some
    writers mistakenly believe that their stories will enjoy
    broader appeal if they generalize the content, for example
    setting the story in an undefined geography. No, no, no!
    Specificity and intimacy with the main character or the
    narrator is what distinguishes a work from those with
    a similar subject matter. Stick to the personal, and the
    universal will take care of itself.

2   *Your voice.* How you tell your story, whether through the
    voice of a character, an authorial storyteller, or yourself as
    narrator, is yet another trait that distinguishes your work.
    Even if you are writing a personal essay, it may take some
    time to find your own unique voice, which I know sounds
    weird. (Whose voice would you write in: Your evil twin's?
    Miss Piggy's?) But language often transmogrifies in its
    journey from head to pen. It can turn stiff like a bad knee.
    It may affect an accent for no good reason. It often has a
    tendency to storm the page in an attack of overwriting.
    No matter. Because when you do settle into the voice of
    your story, you will *own* that material, and don't let any of
    those other talking stones tell you otherwise. I love how
    Grace Paley puts it. "If you say what's on your mind in the
    language that comes to you from your parents and your
    street and friends, you'll probably say something beautiful."

3   *The future of civilization.* The divisiveness that threatens
to destroy life as we know it could be vanquished if only
everyone would sit down with a good book. But don't
take the word of an English major. This news comes from
neuroscientists who have shown that stories allow us to
have surrogate experiences that our brains process almost
identically to lived experiences. In other words, reading
literature does not just enhance our knowledge base,
vocabulary, and conversation skills; it also fosters empathy
and self-awareness, which in turn stimulates our brains to
the degree that it actually changes how we interact in life.
As a writer, your real or imagined stories can provide
those same benefits. At its best, storytelling is a form of
activism, a means of raising a reader's emotional quotient
and connecting people across humanity. Too often, creative
types are labeled indulgent or selfish, because of the time
writing takes away from other demands. Memoirists have it
worse, often having to fend off accusations of navel-gazing.
*Maybe if she'd stop thinking about the meaning behind two
creamers in her coffee, she'd manage to get her kids to school
on time.* Yes, writing requires a degree of self-absorption,
and it can get out of hand. Regardless, Wallace Stegner said
it best: "Writing is a *social* act. An act of communication
both intellectual and emotional. It is also, at its best, an
act of affirmation—a way of joining the human race and a
human culture."

4   *The color blue.* Research suggests that human beings did not
see the color blue before modern times because there was
no word for it. Or, more accurately, they probably saw it
as we do now, but they never really noticed it. In fact, the
Egyptians were the first to coin a word for the color blue,
maybe because theirs was the only culture at the time that
could produce blue dyes. From there, the awareness of the
color spread throughout the modern world.

The claim that a culture with no word for a color cannot see it is supported by a contemporary study with the Himba tribe in Namibia, whose language has several words for nuanced shades of green, but nothing to describe blue. When shown a screen with eleven green squares and one distinctly blue square, the Namibians could not pick out the blue one. Yet, among the green squares that appear identical to a Westerner's eye, they could immediately identify the different shade. The ability to see or not see a shade speaks to its importance to a culture. Now just imagine if every culture had the ability to see every kind of color!

As a writer, your life is the color blue. Your stories are nuances of green. All the things that only you have to offer from your imagination, your experiences, and your unique voice can add those hues to the palette of humanity. You have only to give them words, and what was absent before becomes visible to you and your readers.

So there you have it, four rational responses to the question, Why does your writing matter? The problem is, however, that when the question is actually on the table, the answer is driven much more by emotional rather than rational motives. I am sure, for example, that all of us care deeply about the existence of humankind, but not for a second do I believe that a tagline with the promise, "Write Your Book: Save the World!" provides enough motivation to keep at it, not when a So-and-So is thrown in your face, even by a well-meaning person. And when I say a well-meaning person, this time I am referring to me. Just recently I ambushed an accomplished poet in my community, telling her that her work reminded me of that of the author Naomi Shihab Nye. The woman's expression was the same as if she had run over a chipmunk. She told me that Nye was an author whose work had always made her own feel irrelevant, given that their poetry traversed similar emotional and cultural terrain.

Truly, I had meant my comment as a compliment. What I was trying to say is that I experience the same type of satisfaction after reading each writer's works. How was I supposed to know that Naomi Shihab Nye was this person's So-and-So? The noted author is a friend of a friend. I had heard that she is a very nice person.

In your moments of doubt about writing, I wish I could talk some sense into you. I wish the rational benefits I just provided would be convincing enough to help you cross the threshold to your own writing center. But all I can do is share my personal experience, with the hope that it will inspire you to find your own reasons to keep going when you want to give up.

Why do I write? There have been times, plenty of times, when I have asked myself that question and could not think of a single reason to keep putting words on the page. Even when I have been lucky enough to have a book contract, I have experienced my own moment-of-truth-moments where I imagined myself picking up the phone, calling my editor, saying I quit. My checkbook could accommodate the return of the advance, a fact that speaks more to the modesty of the advance than the health of my bank balance. In those moments, the fantasy of not writing seems so real. A burden lifts. My anxiety dissipates. The feeling of freedom is palpable, no more stomach clenching, no more fear, or self-doubt, or jealousy.

But then it comes back, that refrain in my head. *I have something to say! I have something to say!* That is the reason I wanted to be a writer in the first place; and that is the reason I return to my desk, even when I do not want to go. I am a writer, in good times and bad. This is my identity, my voice, my way of feeling human and heard. When it gradually sinks in what not writing would really mean, that's when my feelings of relief turn to anxiety and then panic. *Who would I be if I weren't a writer? How will people know all the things I need to tell them? Plus, I have no hobbies, so what would I do with all that free time?* And so my decision to write comes down to a reason that is not just emotional, but clearly neurotic. I write because the thought of not writing makes me feel worse than the worst I have ever felt when I am writing.

Why should you write? Why does it matter? How do you convince yourself to not give up during the bad times, when that is exactly what you want to do? I could remind you that you have a unique perspective and voice, because you do. I could argue that your stories can foster understanding, and empathy, and make the world a better place. I could even tell you that your words have the power to turn the sky blue, and this would not be a lie. In the end, however, the only answer that counts, the only reason to keep writing that really matters, is the one that makes perfect sense to you.

I Write Because . . .

Why Does Your Writing Matter? Take the time to put
down on paper why writing matters to you. What do
you get out of it? How does it make you feel? Keep this
paper close at hand to ward off your So-and-Sos, real
and imagined.

A Walk around the Block

It is a dubious distinction to be invited to participate in a panel discussion about writer's block, but there I was, seated with two other "experts" in front of an expectant audience. I told the story of my worst case of writer's block, a time not so long ago when I struggled to come back to my work after a long dry spell. My enthusiasm for every new idea quickly fizzled out. I could not hear my voice. One day, I found myself struggling to remember the keystrokes that formed the apostrophe symbol. That is when I fled my desk for a nearby café and started writing . . .

It was just after nine on a Thursday morning, so the normal-job people had come and gone, giving way to stragglers like me who treated the café as their personal office. I sat at the end of a long center table littered with sections of the local newspaper.

"Mind if I sit here?" The question came from a weathered garden gnome of a man wearing a flannel shirt cinched into baggy jeans. He pointed to a seat at the other end of my table.

"No, of course not." I had seen him before, a friendly old-timer around town.

The man glanced at the headlines. Party politics. Name-calling. Scandal. And this was just in the local section of the paper. "Fine day," he said, without a trace of irony.

Turkish novelist Orhan Pamuk, who won the Nobel Prize in Literature in 2006, shared the following advice in his Nobel lecture: "To become a writer, patience and toil are not enough: we must first feel compelled to escape crowds, company, the stuff of ordinary, everyday life . . . the desire to shut oneself up in a room is what pushes us into action." Pamuk reemphasized this idea: "The starting point of true literature is the man who shuts himself up in his room with his books."

This is indeed a popularized ideal, writers escaping into quietude, keeping company with other people's words as a way to inspire their own thoughts and stories. Pamuk grew up in a large family, so I suspect peace and quiet were rare luxuries in his childhood. As a young man, he studied architecture and journalism and also had ambitions to be an artist, but at age twenty-three he decided to become a novelist, and so, according to his biography, he retreated to his flat in Istanbul and began to write.

I cannot argue with Pamuk's success or literary prowess, but his statement about the starting point of true literature stopped me. To my ear, such a declaration makes the creative process sound too, too . . . what? *Precious* is the descriptor that eventually came to mind. For most writers, our work is already precious, literally of great value to us, not to be treated carelessly. So I think this prescription to avoid the ordinary does not always serve, especially if the air around our writing desks becomes so rarefied we find it hard to breathe.

Let me back up a moment. Of course there are times when we require long stretches of solitude to do our work, and reading other authors serves to teach and inspire us. A good many days I cannot wait to shut the door to the turquoise-colored room of my study, and start the workday by reading passages from favorite worn-covered books. But based on personal experience, and what so many others have told me, there are just as many days when the company of literature can be downright off-putting. I think of a woman who recently joined one of my workshops. She is in her late twenties and works at the customer service desk at Walmart. She told me that she used to love to write, but the genius of Virginia Woolf did her in. "I thought, I'll never be able to write like her," the young woman said, "and then I got writer's block and quit." I think this is a common conundrum for aspiring authors. Books feed our soul and desire to write, but those same books can be our undoing at certain stages of the learning curve. How do we reach that level of mastery? How can we discern the process that will get us from here to there? Artists go to great care to hide the brushstrokes, to purge all signs of struggle in the finished work. So for frangible writers, even a library of one can loom so large that it breaks our creative spirit.

In his lecture, Pamuk refers to the French Renaissance philosopher and essayist Montaigne, whom he notes as the precursor of this sort of writer who shuts himself away for long periods to read and reflect. Credited for popularizing the essay as a literary genre, Montaigne is also famously known for his motto, "*Que sais-je?*" Translation: What do I know? As a skeptic, Montaigne recognized that he and his fellow philosophers actually understood very little about the world, and therefore he strove instead for self-knowledge, dwelling on his personal thoughts, feelings, and experiences.

What do I know? This is the question that confronts all writers sitting alone at their desks, trying to figure out something meaningful or engaging to put on the page. Sometimes, we cannot wait to start typing to discover the answer. When we are really on fire, it feels like we are conversing with some remarkably engaging and deeper version of ourselves. Fiction writers in this state of heightened creativity often report that it feels like they are channeling their characters. But when we are struggling, what we hear in response to that question is silence, silence, and then a more prolonged, deafening silence.

Que sais-je?

Que sais-je?

Que sais-je?

I admit I have never been good at foreign languages, but I believe that is how you say "writer's block" in French.

Some people argue that there is no such thing as writer's block, but I think those people lack empathy and imagination. (I threw in the latter because imagination is required to feel empathy.) My own belief is that writer's block is not only real, but real-er than real because it is a metaphor that gives density to an abstraction. Therefore, trying to overcome it can make us feel like we are trapped inside the following brainteaser: A writer goes to a surgeon and tells her a giant block is lodged inside his head. He wants it gone! It has come to weigh so much that when he sits at his desk, he often has to support his head in his hands. The surgeon can see the toll this block has taken on the writer—his entire demeanor appears to be weighted down—so she agrees to remove it immediately. But after surgery, the doctor says to the writer, "I'm sorry, but when I looked inside your head, it was empty."

Exactly. How do we dislodge a physical abstraction?

Most people who are suffering from writer's block try to confront it head-on. Think! Think! Think! I need a brilliant idea! A scintillating storyline! A memory worthy of a reflective essay! I believe a good deal of the blame for all this thinking can be attributed to the fact that writers are often burdened with a degree in the liberal arts, or at least we share liberal arts sensibilities. The very purpose of such a broad-based, book-fed education is to enhance our capacity to think or, more specifically, to develop and hone our critical thinking skills. Unfortunately, however, when it comes to writer's block, the only thing worse than thinking is critical thinking. We analyze and discard ideas before they have the opportunity to play out. We make judgments of our work before it hits the page. And the more thoughts we think but fail to give expression, the more compacted they become in our heads. Meanwhile, the authors we have shut ourselves in with check their timepieces and chain-smoke Gauloises, making it even harder to breathe the thin air.

A woman, her hair in long braids, came into the café and stopped by our table to chat with the old man. I did not know her personally, but I recognized her from the ads she runs for her yoga practice. I also knew that her ex was dating a friend of mine, and the other week I had seen her buying a curious amount of chicken wire at the lumberyard. In a small town like mine, this is how you do not know someone.

"My brother passed away last week," my tablemate told the woman after they had covered the weather and other issues of small talk. "Eleven of us kids," he added, "and now it's down to just me." This news was jarring. He had seemed so . . . unburdened.

"Let me buy you a corn muffin," the yoga instructor insisted, heading to the counter over the old man's protests. Her kindness made me want to wear my hair in braids.

A café. A conversation. A corn muffin. During my worst case of writer's block, this was the stuff that marked my return to the page. But what else did I have to write about, except what was right there in front of me? With no ideas of my own, I needed to get outside my own head. I needed to stop thinking so hard. As it turns out, what I really needed was a distraction.

So much has been written about the dangers of distraction to writers. The Internet, most notably, can disrupt our concentration in ways that cost us creatively. But before we shut ourselves away too tightly, let us revisit Virginia Woolf for a moment, with her call for a room of one's own. Woolf's words are a rallying cry for writers beleaguered by demands on their time and attention, but it is worth noting that the room of our own that she asks us to conjure up is one "like many thousands, with a window looking across people's hats and vans and motor-cars to other windows." In fact, writers have always sought connection with the world to gather ideas and spark creativity. When we experience writer's block, one of the issues may be that we misguidedly shut off these channels of creativity that allow for free association and mind wandering, both of which are critical for inspiration.

There is a saying that life is what happens when we are busy making other plans. It has occurred to me that a variation of that insight might be useful in understanding a possible solution to writer's block—writing is what happens when we are busy looking away from the page. Certainly, this is what happened to me when my plan was to stare down the computer until I came up with a brilliant idea, but what actually happened was that I found my way back to the craft by hanging out in a café. The young woman who works at Walmart provides a similar testimonial. She overcame her block not by fixating on her desire to write as well as Virginia Woolf, but via a random writing exercise in one of my workshops. I cannot remember the actual prompt, but I do remember that this young woman developed from it a short piece about her job that hinted at remarkable talent. After witnessing this woman's return to writing, I would like to amend Pamuk's pronouncement about the starting point of true literature. Yes, it could be a man who shuts himself up in a room with his books. But it is just as likely to be a woman who works the customer service desk of Walmart, where there is no escape from crowds, and what pushes her into action is some customer who insists on getting his money back for a returned air mattress, even though he has lost the receipt.

Of course you don't need to hightail it to a small-town café, or work at a big-box store, to overcome writer's block. Helpful distractions are everywhere, as long as you assume a different kind of attention and discipline. In *The Art of Fiction*, Henry James offered this advice to writers: "Try to be one of the people on whom nothing is lost!" This strikes me as a noble but exhausting goal, so I have modified James's advice to something more proportionate to my abilities: take note of what you notice.

My feeling is that we just happen to attend to certain particulars—rather than the countless other particulars that fall within
our immediate sensory realm—for reasons that may not be apparent, but that serve our creative process. Just look around. So
many details could stop our eye, and yet we take note of . . . ?
*There! A film of dust on the windowsill. But didn't you just wipe that
sill the other day? Or maybe you haven't cleaned for weeks? Regardless, your neighbors are to blame for your dusty house, thanks to the
addition they are building onto their home. Every day you have to endure the noise of earthmovers and the detritus of construction floating
in the air. Why are some people so obsessed with having more space?
Why do they feel bigger is better? When you were a kid, your parents
moved your family to a big, fancy house, and that's when all the fighting started . . .*

Can you see in this example how taking note of what you notice
launches the creative process? First, you react (dust). Second, you
respond (frustration turning to anger). Third, as your brain forms
associations (from the neighbor's new addition to your childhood
home), you make a leap toward meaningful material. I suspect
that when we have writer's block, we are trying so hard to make
that creative leap that we sometimes forget about those first two
steps necessary for leverage. As Allen Ginsberg once said, "The
ordinary is made extraordinary by your attention to it."

Here is another type of useful distraction, one more applicable
to writers who are already involved in a project but stuck in the
development stage. I am talking about "writing outside the story,"
which could mean rummaging through the back of a character's
closet, or making a list of her top ten bad habits, or journaling
about something that befuddles you, like how those bakeries that
sell only fancy cupcakes stay in business. (I cannot imagine how
cupcakes can turn a decent profit.)

I bet I know what you are thinking right now because it is probably the same thing I used to think when people told me to write

about cupcakes. *Like I have that kind of time.* My nature prefers efficiency, so writing outside the story—knowing that whatever I come up with is unlikely to fit tidily in the narrative proper—just seemed like more wasted time and energy. Since then, however, I have learned that this practice often expedites the creative process. For fiction writers, writing outside the story is a great way to get to know your characters, including the secrets they have been trying to protect from you. (Just think about the items you have buried in the back of your own closet.) For writers of creative nonfiction, this can help you access your voice. When I am struggling in my work, the voice that emerges tends toward that of Mr. Howell, the pompous British millionaire on Gilligan's Island. Yet when I warm up by writing outside of any narrative structure, I quickly come to sound more like myself, which I prefer to believe is the opposite of Mr. Howell.

> The old man stood and brushed some muffin crumbs from his shirtfront. "Thank you for sharing this table," he said to me. His smile revealed two stalwart bottom teeth, facing off like boxers across a gap of gum. I gave him a quick smile in return. Imagine, having all those brothers and sisters, and now being the only one left. I watched him leave the café, bent by age but, remarkably, not by life.

Toward the end of the panel discussion on writer's block, someone in the audience asked me what happened to that stuff I wrote about in the café. Was it useable? Did any of it end up in anything that mattered? I could have said yes, because here is a bit of it in this chapter, which matters greatly to me. But that would have been missing the point. *Que sais-je?*

What I know is that I wish I had said the same thing in return to the old man—*Thank you for sharing this table.* It seems counterintuitive to put our faith in distraction as a means to a meaningful end, especially when so much of the time our progress depends on our ability to do exactly the opposite—shut out distraction. So it can be hard not to try to think, think, think our way through writer's block. But if our liberal arts sensibilities have burdened us with an abundance of critical thinking skills,* they also have equipped us with the ability to see solutions that are beyond the obvious, even paradoxical.

The creative process is too much of a mystery to trace precisely how those few hours in the café inspired the words that came next, and next, and next. But thanks to that experience, I also know that sometimes the only way to get back to our precious writing is to focus on what is truly precious. And that is life. Ordinary, everyday life. If we cannot confront writer's block head-on, then maybe we can simply walk around it, and appreciate the people and the stories we notice along the way.

*In case my comments have mislead readers, let the record show that I believe a liberal arts education is a great thing, and I am not aligned in any way with those right-wing politicians who love to trash the humanities, and who push legislation to end programs and grants to college students interested in studying "poetry or some other Pre-Walmart major," to quote from one legislator's email. I do believe it is wrong that anyone should have to borrow $40,000 to major in anything, but if I had to assume that degree of debt, I would not consider it a waste of money to acquire, for example, an understanding of Greek philosophy, or history, or even English literature.

Heart to Heart

Most Mondays, I lead an expressive writing workshop for parolees and other past offenders, organized by the restorative justice program in my community. Expressive writing is personal and emotional writing without regard to form. The format in this workshop is similar to what I imagine happens in most expressive writing groups. I offer a prompt, and, for a timed period, people write about whatever the exercise evokes. The prompt is not the point—you do not need to start with an assigned topic—but the device does set a direction, and gives the writer an *in*, a way to start forming word associations, unleash thoughts and feelings, and tap into meaningful memories and stories.

I recall one particular class, when five participants showed up for the workshop, four of them regulars to the group, plus one newcomer I will call Jasmine. We gathered around the small table near a poster offering tips on how to make restitution, and I gave the writing prompt, *This keeps me sane.* About fifteen minutes later, I invited everyone to share what they had written. Jasmine read last, but stopped short when she reached her final sentence.

"I can't say shit like that aloud." She fidgeted in her chair, her nervousness erupting in machine-gun laughter.

"Are you sure?" I asked her, halfheartedly. I did not want to push too hard because I didn't know anything about Jasmine, or what was in the pocket of her camo jacket.

"It's really bad. Serious shit." More rat-a-tat-tat laughter.

"Just read the fucking thing," said Laurie, a lovely person and regular in the group who shows a remarkably positive attitude in the wake of three years in jail, a degenerative disease, and a hellish mother. She yanked Jasmine's notebook out of her hands and read the last line for her: "Wait, I wanna kill. Wait, I gotta chill."

"You see," Laurie smiled at Jasmine, "You can say things like that in here."

It occurred to me at the time that I should discourage yanking in my workshops, but it happens so rarely. Plus, I knew Laurie meant the gesture kindly, and that is what counts.

We talked about Jasmine's piece for a short spell, what we noticed or liked about it, what it evoked in us. I especially liked the sentence, "I walk down the street in my imagination, helping out, doing little things." It made me think, mostly about how easily I stereotype people wearing camo. Once again, I was reminded that people are so much more than what they initially project. All in all, this was a typical, meaningful workshop experience, except for the fact that Will, a professional rock guitarist who had recently discovered that he could play a gig even without being wasted, was not wearing his sunglasses for some reason.

Later, as I was leaving the office of restorative justice, I heard Jasmine ask the program director if she could come back to our group the following week. This made me feel good, and reaffirmed one of the key benefits of expressive writing. It is always gratifying when you reveal what really goes on in your head, and see how other people you had assumed were normal can relate to your craziest thoughts. There is comfort in that, knowing that no one is normal.

The remarkable value of expressive writing came to light thanks in large part to the research of social psychologist James W. Pennebaker, now chair of the department of psychology at the University of Texas at Austin. In his 1990 book *Opening Up: The Healing Power of Confiding in Others*, he described this special kind of writing to deal with traumatic events or emotionally difficult situations. One might think that dredging up repressed feelings and reliving bad life experiences would make most people feel worse or intensify negative emotions, but Pennebaker found just the opposite to be true. In the aftermath of writing about emotion-laden subjects—specifically linking events and feelings—people's spirits lifted considerably and their physical health improved. The benefits of expressive writing, also referred to as reflective or introspective writing, range from increased control and creativity to decreased anxiety, depression, and rage. The more detailed the written account, the greater the emotional and physical payoffs.

In his research, Pennebaker found that the positive effects of expressive writing do not depend on outsiders reading your words or offering any responses. No wonder so many people take the time to commit their most visceral feelings to private journals. My experience, however, speaks to the added value of expressing yourself on the page within a supportive community. I know human nature is such that we often feel safer keeping certain thoughts to ourselves for fear of being judged. But sometimes the least safe place for our secrets is in our own heads.

Occasionally, I ask people in my various groups, "Why do you come here to write?"

"To be a better person."

"To learn what I'm thinking."

"Things need to be written down."

"To be friends with myself."

"When you make your story public, it relieves some of the pain."

One time after a workshop at the restorative justice program, I overheard Will, the guitarist with the sunglasses, say to another participant, "Good, now I'm done with all the shit I have to do today." Because attendance is voluntary, and Will rarely missed a class, his comment took me by surprise.

"Is that how you see this workshop?" I asked him, "as something you have to do?"

"You know what I mean," he responded. "I have to do it for me."

From my perspective as the workshop facilitator, just the fact that these people show up and write, and share their writing and responses with others, suggests that each participant is a more evolved human being than he or she might think.

Because of its power to help writers deal more effectively with difficult issues, expressive writing workshops are often advertised as writing for healing. That sounds fine coming from other workshop facilitators, but not coming from me. For years, I made a point to stick to leading groups for fiction and creative nonfiction writers that focused solely on narrative craft. Craft! Craft! Craft! I happen to love discussing issues of narrative craft, but this focus also kept me a safe distance from dealing with feelings. "Yes, I realize the deathbed scene of the beloved grandfather is important to the novel, but the pacing drags and the dialogue is stilted. And, please, stop weeping. It's affecting my concentration."

My view was that it was hard enough to be around myself in a bad mood, thus I could not imagine what it would be like to be trapped in a room full of other emotional writers. Luckily, however, that very opportunity presented itself to me about seven years ago, when a woman in my community proposed that one of the offerings at my writer's center include a workshop in the form of a women's writing circle. As she described it, women would gather as a group, write, and share their truths.

"An excellent idea!" I responded, knowing that some people like this kind of thing. "Send along a description of the workshop, and let me know when you want to run it."

"Oh no," the woman said. "I don't want to run the group. I think you would be a better workshop facilitator."

Me? What did I know of dealing with people's feelings? For that matter, what did I know of writing for self-awareness? On my bookshelf sits a tall stack of lovely journals that I have been gifted over the years, all just waiting to be regifted. Regardless, the woman's flattery—and perhaps some previously dormant instinct from the better part of my self—trumped my misgivings and lack of credentials. So, there I was a few months later, sitting in a circle of eight women of different ages and from diverse backgrounds, all writing from a prompt, and sharing their words about life, love, laughter, and loss.

What happened then? I think of that first meeting of the women's writing circle as my "Grinch Moment," specifically the moment in the story when the Grinch watches all the Whos down in Whoville, recently robbed of their Christmas accoutrements, and yet there they all are, singing in a circle, heart to heart and hand to hand. In the story, the Grinch's heart grew three sizes that day, and I think my heart grew, too, witnessing the candor and connection in that circle of women. I admire anyone who has the courage to come to a workshop and share her writing. But sharing our personal lives on the page, and then exposing our stories, thoughts, and feelings to others, without any pretty packaging or time to edit—that takes the kind of gumption and generosity I need to be around. I want some to rub off on me.

Over the years, I have continued to lead expressive writing groups for women and men, at my writer's center and through a variety of social services programs, at executive education conferences, at universities and veterans' programs, and anywhere else I am lucky enough to be invited. I cannot remember an instance when these workshops did not leave me feeling uplifted. This is not because the subject matter is fun—hardly—but because at every meeting, the participants who show up remind me of the triumph of the human spirit. Just the other day I was in a workshop of survivors of domestic violence that started with one woman sharing a gut-wrenching memory of how her former partner terrorized her, and ended with all of us (okay, almost all of us) agreeing that we should go zip-lining as a group.

For people like me, that is, authors of nonfiction and fiction who write with regard to form, expressive writing can play a vital role in our creative lives. Free of the shackles of narrative craft, released from the burden of attending to correct spelling and grammar, unrestricted by anything including page margins, freewriting is a great way to turn on the tap of our creative juices. From what I have witnessed in workshops, it is almost impossible to freewrite for more than a few minutes without running headlong into meaningful material. This practice also serves to help warm up your voice, and offers a detour around judgment. Whenever your words stop flowing and devolve into something . . . something . . . something . . . freewriting provides a great go-to for inspiration.

Recently, I was chatting up a poet who owns a café named Dream. He told me that he freewrites in his journal as soon as he wakes up in the morning, which did not take me by surprise because, really, how could a poet–café owner with a business named Dream not keep a journal?

"Why?" I asked him, because I am still trying to convince myself to adopt this daily practice.

"Because when I look back at what I wrote six months ago, I can see how it has affected what I am doing now."

His answer reminded me of yet another benefit of freewriting, which is that the very act of writing has an inherent value, even when the outcome is raw or unusable in our manuscripts. For me, who still aspires to keeping a journal, the closest parallel is my daily practice of creating a to-do list, and including as the first item, "Make a to-do list!" In this way, I can check off a bit of progress almost immediately, and start my day with a sense of accomplishment.

Maybe because I prefer to think in terms of "to-do" rather than "to-dwell," I suspect that some of my earlier resistance to conducting expressive writing workshops related to how they are frequently packaged. "Writing for healing." "Writing for recovery."

"Storytelling Interventions." The last is what some academic in-
stitutions call these initiatives aimed at helping at-risk college students internalize positive messages, such as a sense of belonging.
To my ear, those words—healing, recovery, intervention—sound
so deficit oriented, suggesting that whoever engages in this practice clearly needs to be fixed. Indeed, we are all broken at times.
But based on the participants I have met in my groups, I think
more promissory descriptors are in order. "Writing for kickass
change!" "Writing to show that you rock!" "Writing for joy!"

Perhaps such exclamatory language would scare people away
from a class. I recall an experience my upbeat friend Becky shared
with me about the time she struggled to enact a new initiative
at the university where she works as a high-level administrator.
She heard through the grapevine this comment from a colleague:
"Clearly, Becky knows what she's talking about, but I just can't
handle her enthusiasm." Despite cautionary tales like this, I still
would prefer a descriptor that better captures this potential for
positive transformation.

I think of Stephanie, once quiet and lacking confidence, and
how she found an apartment for herself and her little boy, and got
the courts to deny all parental rights to the boy's abusive father. I
witnessed this journey through her writing over the course of several workshops.

I think of Keith, who convinced himself, first on the page,
and then in real life, to quit smoking, the last of his long line of
addictions.

I think of Grace, who had been contemplating suicide during
a sexual harassment lawsuit that cost her a marriage and a good
job, and yet she found the courage to share her writing in a local
theater performance by survivors of abuse. "It was," she told our
group, "the most amazing experience of my life."

I think of Jessie, whose story echoes way too many other wom-
en's stories. During one workshop, she revealed a secret that was

literally making her sick, that she had been raped by a relative when she was a young teenager. Sitting beside Jessie on that day was Louise, a newcomer at our meetings. Louise was fighting stage IV breast cancer, and appeared as fragile as a sapling in body, but not in spirit. "I'm a hugger," Louise told Jessie after hearing her story. "Would you like me to give you a hug?"

In my former career as a more emotionally stunted workshop leader, those words would have evoked in me a wave of nervous anxiety, which I probably would have countered with a lengthy lecture on how to craft a topic sentence. But if expressive writing teaches us anything, it is that people are not immutable. We do not have to be stuck in our past, or in our current situation. We do not have to be stuck in old patterns of thinking and feeling. When we make a practice of putting down on paper our truths, without censorship or second-guessing, we gain clarity about who we are in the moment, and the genesis of how we arrived there. With this clarity comes the opportunity for awareness, acceptance, change, and growth.

That day in the workshop, when Louise gave Jessie a hug, I swear I was *this close* to vaulting from my chair in the circle and throwing my arms around both of them. Thank goodness I did not, because I probably would have flattened frail Louise, though, in mental fortitude, I am sure she could take me any day of the week. Still, to have such an impulse speaks to my own potential for kickass change. Rather than avoiding feelings, I now look forward to keeping company with a roomful of emotional writers, all of us, including me, heart to heart and hand to hand. The people in my expressive writing groups have helped me evolve as a teacher, a writer, and a person. They also haven given me hope that maybe, one day, I will see all those lovely journals stacked on my shelf, and I will recognize them for the gifts they are, as I read about my own thoughts and feelings expressed on each page, with no thought of form or craft, and no room left in the margins.

Decluttering

"You've ruined reading for me."

If I've heard that comment once, I've heard it a thousand times from people who have taken my workshops. Always, I feel flattered and reassured that I am doing my job.

The process of learning to write well can take considerable time, and in fact we are never really done learning, given how the next story presents new challenges. As Eudora Welty put it, "Each story tells me how to write it, but not the one afterwards." Reading well, on the other hand, has a shorter learning curve. The following is a fictionalized account of what typically occurs after a writer has completed just one six-week workshop.

After being inundated with narrative craft, the workshop graduate looks forward to getting back to reading for pleasure. A few pages into her bedside book, however, she stumbles upon an unnecessary adverb—"Rudely, he interrupted his date." *Oh, puh-leeze!* she thinks. The workshop graduate no longer has patience for this kind of bad behavior in writing or life, so she plucks another book from her shelf. Within the first chapter she encounters a bloated description, a mixed metaphor, and—*Are you frigging kidding me?*—a jarring point-of-view shift.

Abandoning her own library, she hurries to the bookstore where she beelines to that new best seller she has been dying to read. *A best seller has to be well written*, she thinks, as she begins to skim the first chapter.

The girl's mouth formed a large O . . .

Her mind wandered to the back of the closet . . .

> She found herself dancing in a field of fluttering
> butterflies when the alarm clock sounded . . .

Ruined! Ruined forever this book and now every other poorly written, hastily produced, insufficiently edited book that she used to consume with the same degree of pleasure as eating one of those soft after-dinner mints offered in diners. *I mean, they tasted sort of good, so who cared if they left a filmy residue on your tongue?* The workshop graduate returns the new best seller to the display table and heads to the "Literature" section of the bookstore. She feels at once reluctant and eager, as understanding sinks in—this is the dawn of a new age of reading, where point of view will never again simply mean a person's opinion.

I remember that sense of loss as a reader. Early in my creative writing education, I returned to my childhood home to visit my parents, and picked up a well-worn copy of *Wicked Loving Lies* from my bookshelf. How could I have never noticed before how the word "loins" looks really weird on the page, especially if you stare at it too long?

The world is full of bad books, and although I support self-publishing as a form of democratization, it has only exacerbated the situation. Thankfully, however, an equal number of beautifully written books exist from both traditional and self-publishers across genres. So if an awareness of craft has undermined your pleasure in reading bad writing, take heart that it has conversely enhanced your pleasure in reading good writing. What a gift it is to have heightened literary sensibilities, or heightened sensibilities in any artistic realm—painting, cooking, music. "Oh my goodness, Just listen to how the guitarist used the unison bend to produce that sustained note *sans vibrato*. A perfect tension release!" Even as you are transported by a song, or painting, or soufflé, or story, the experience is enriched by your awareness of the techniques employed to achieve such mastery, at least to the degree that any worthy work gives up its secrets.

As writers, we are blessed to have such second sight, but with it comes a responsibility to our own artistic integrity. Think about all those times you finished reading a published work and thought, *I could write a better book than that!* Remember this as you seek publication for your efforts. You do not want to be the author some other writer thinks that about.

I come from a family with a rich heritage of maniacal housekeeping. For years, my mother and older sisters tried to convince me of the satisfaction, even pleasure, that comes from vacuuming, scrubbing, and dusting. Because I despise housework, I always considered myself a black sheep in this regard, until I realized that I do share this predilection; it just manifests on the page rather than in my home. How I love a clean manuscript! I love the transformational power of editing. As writers, our work is rooted in the conventional characters of the alphabet. Those characters form words. Those words form language. Our job is to form meaning with that language, which ultimately requires scrutinizing every noun, verb, pronoun, and article, and the arrangement of those elements in every sentence. Deconstructed in this way, writing, and specifically editing, can sound tedious and terrifying, but the rewards that can come from even our smallest efforts are remarkable! Just the other day, I scrubbed the word "very" from a sentence. You have no idea how happy that "little" change made me. Or maybe you do. I hope you do.

"I don't like editing." I have heard plenty of writers voice this sentiment. Of course, they are entitled to their opinion, as long as it is not used to justify subjecting innocent readers to their sloppy work. Another comment I hear from writers on a regular basis is, "I don't want to edit because it could mess up what's already working." Or this iteration: "I don't want to overwork the story." If I were a lawyer, these arguments would be part of what I would call the Slippery Slope Defense, a strategy employed by people across realms who want to get out of doing something good that might take a little effort or disrupt the status quo. *If you allow one edit in, it could lead to a whole bunch of other edits wanting to get in, and there goes the manuscript.* My editorial integrity disinclines me from using this defense in my work, but not in my life. Just the other day, I decided not to volunteer at a bake sale because if I did, I reasoned, the organizers would then be after me all the time for my Betty Crocker brownies.

I wish I could reassure writers that when they edit, there is no chance they will "mess up what is already working" in their manuscripts. But by definition, editing means cutting, rearranging, revamping our tidy, but flawed word packages for the greater good. To effectively revise a passage or sentence, we must call on our instincts and acquired knowledge of editing techniques, but also submit to a good deal of trial and error. It is inevitable that sometimes we will move our language in the wrong direction, at least temporarily. That said, the experience of editing my own work, and witnessing the process through countless workshop participants and writing clients, has shown me that, on average, the ratio of missteps to moving in the right direction is 1:12. And, worst-case scenario, if you do find that you have overworked your story with too many fusses and tweaks, well, that is why you save your previous drafts.

Writing is rewriting. You have probably heard that expression before, and goodness knows I have repeated it enough in my teaching practice, instilling dread in myself and everyone else around me. Sometimes, though, I think such a pithy assessment actually sugarcoats the workload, or at least raises the possibility of misleading us into believing that creative writing is a two-step process: (1) Scribble something down. (2) Revise. I suppose that covers the gist of our workload, but it fails to highlight, or distinguish, the editing process as its own phase, unique in many ways from two of the phases that precede it—drafting and revision. One could argue that editing is simply a subset of the revision phase, but here I am talking about editing for language, not structure. Call it line editing, or copyediting, or something less printable, but the pace of this later stage of scrutiny differs from that of revising to shape the prose. Editing requires that we lean in close to every sentence, every word, every punctuation mark. We must adjust our focus to a macro lens to draw attention to the magic of the ordinary. Maybe because editing follows the heavy lifting of drafting and structural revision, this is the part of the writing process that most often gets short shrift. A fitting analogy might be to compare the editing phase to the last child in a family of three kids.

"Where's my baby book with my little ink footprint?" the youngest asks. "Why aren't there any photographs of my first haircut? Come to think of it, where is the footage of me graduating from Harvard or accepting the Nobel Peace Prize?"

"I'm sorry," one or both parents reply, "but those other two kids ran us ragged, so we just stopped giving a shit."

Really now, is that any excuse?

Given that the phrase "writing is rewriting" might not be strong enough to motivate reluctant self-editors, I advocate rewording it for the sake of clarity, and to better manage expectations. My suggestion is the following: Writing is rewriting 41,000 drafts.

I recognize that the idea of having to go through 41,000 drafts before calling a piece done could be off-putting to some writers. *My goodness, I'm not sure I'm up for that. Plus, I am in my late eighties.* There are upsides, however, to framing the writing process in such extreme terms. For example, it would stop writers from beating themselves up so much. *I'm the slowest writer in the world. It takes me forever to finish a piece.* How many times have you felt this way? Writing, particularly the editing phase, is supposed to be a thoughtful, often laborious effort, so why not acknowledge that this is the nature of the job, rather than assume you have some kind of personality deficit?

We also can take heart that a good many of those 41,000 drafts will happen in the creative backstretch, after the architecture of your story and scene development are sound. The editing process is likely to unfold somewhat like this: You revise a sentence. Then you delete the revised sentence. Then you press Control Z to restore the revised sentence and revise it again, but it is still not right. Then you take a shower, and the perfect wording comes to you as you are lathering your hair, so you run foam-headed and dripping to your computer and revise the revised, deleted, restored, re-revised sentence one more time. Yes! That is exactly what you were trying to communicate all along. Plus, all that effort counts for at least four drafts, though who is counting in matters of such importance?

The other day in a workshop, we were discussing a draft of a well-organized essay with serviceable writing.

"Good job," I said. "Now you'll just want to do a ton of editing to take it up to the next level."

The writer looked overwhelmed. "Okay, but how do you edit?" she asked. "I mean, do you hire someone to fix your piece?"

Well, there is that option. Every story benefits from having an expert set of eyes look it over. A professional line editor, for example, will address issues related to the creative content, writing style, and language use at the sentence and paragraph level. A copyeditor is more concerned with word usage, rules of grammar, and punctuation. My feeling, however, is that turning a work over to someone with the hope that he will "fix it" runs the risk of giving up too much creative control.

Editing is not just about cleaning up your manuscript; it is a creative process unto itself. The very meaning of your story is carried in its language, its semantics. Mark Twain famously commented, "The difference between the almost right word and the right word is really a large matter—'tis the difference between the lightning-bug and the lightning." This speaks to how word choice can have such a significant impact on our work.

When I write, a good part of my understanding of the piece is enhanced through the editing process. I recall working on the last line edits of an essay that struck me as flat, at best a well-written anecdote. I knew what my piece was about, but not the deeper meaning, the "what about what it was about." As I continued to polish the work, I struggled over one particular sentence in the penultimate paragraph. Finally, in a fit of temper, I stopped trying to be all fancypants with the language, and just wrote in plain English what I was trying to communicate in that sentence. That was the moment when I understood the "what about what it was about," my point, if you will. With this sudden clarity of theme— all thanks to a line edit—I was able to elevate my anecdote into an essay through a surprisingly little amount of further finessing. I think about that experience a lot, especially when I am struggling to communicate something that feels impossible to capture on the page—love, gratitude, loss. People often say, "There are no words," but I have come to realize that there are, as long as they are the right words.

"How do you edit?" When the woman in my workshop asked this question, it took me by surprise. We talk about editing issues all the time in class. Plus, when I looked at her draft, the flaws and missed opportunities flared from the page, but of course it is always easier to spot trouble when you are looking at a manuscript from the outside in. Her question reminded me that, like every phase of the creative process, even editing can feel overwhelming if you focus on the whole. This supports another benefit that comes from acknowledging the reality that writing is rewriting 41,000 drafts. It frees us from the expectation that we are supposed to be able to address every issue in our manuscript at once. That is the kind of pressure that can make us shrink from our work. In fact, editing requires a considerable number of drafts because each iteration uncovers new issues. The process is comparable to entering a disorderly house. At first, you don't even see the smudge of chocolate ice cream on the toy-strewn carpet, but once the house is picked up, that smudge screams for some Woolite rug cleaner.

To make editing a messy manuscript a more palatable, fruitful, satisfying process, it helps to break down the job and single out certain issues to address in each draft. For example, any one of the following common displays of weak writing provide a good focus for your attention:

Anthropomorphized body parts: My head hit the pillow. Her eyes roamed the room. His lips formed a grimace.

Stilted dialogue: "Hello. Would you like me to hang up your coat?" "Yes, thank you for hanging up my coat."

Intrusive dialogue setups: Before she could finish her sentence, he interrupted her, "Do you like your calamari?"

Stage directions: She crossed the room, sat on the couch, looked out the window, and sighed.

Awkward introductory clauses: Racing around the track, Genevieve decided she would order pizza for supper.

As you know, Bobs (dialogue as thinly disguised backstory): "Say, Gillian, would you mind if I borrow that ring that we both know your ex bought you as a clutch move to win you back after you caught him having an affair with his tax accountant?"

Any weird descriptions related to crying or laughing: She cried a
single tear . . . We doubled over in laughter. (Have you ever
seen a person do either of those things in real life? I don't
think so.)

The word "chuckle": (Just because I can't stand that word.)

I could add more categories to this list of common editing opportunities, but I do not need to because, already, there exist numerous, comprehensive self-editing guides for help with style,
readability, grammar, and overall better writing. What I do want
to encourage here, though, is a philosophy of editing that can
make this meaningful process even more meaningful. In her
mega-selling book *The Life-Changing Magic of Tidying Up*, Marie
Kondo offers this advice about decluttering. When you are decid-
ing whether to save or toss something, hold it in your hands. Ask
yourself, is this item useful? Does it spark joy? If the answer to
both questions is no, get rid of it, but purge with respect.

I am already a world-class declutterer. I throw things out from
under people even as they are using them. "Wait, I wasn't done
reading that newspaper!" Still, I believe Kondo's philosophy applied to our writing lives could add a little life-changing magic
to the editing process. It's so easy to vilify our wrong words, or
be embarrassed by them. Yet, with a more gracious approach to
decluttering our manuscripts, we could stop disparaging the language in our drafts that no longer serves or sparks joy, and let it go
with appreciation for the role it did play in our creative process.

Draft 40,998 . . . 40,999 . . . 41,000! There comes a day finally,
thankfully, when you make your last edit, and think, hope, pray
you are done. Writers often ask, "How do you know when a piece
is finished?" My guess is that it works this way: You put away your
"finished" work for a spell to get some distance from it. Then, on a
day when you are in a good frame of mind, you reread it. Nothing

glitches your ear or fumbles your tongue. You review it again, this time reading random passages aloud. The syntax is smooth, the words precise, and the prose rhythm underscores your intent. If you are a proofreader, you read it backwards, just to catch every word. Then you wait a few more days, and read it again. If, during this reading, your nose stings a little, even though you are normally not a crier, that is when you know you are done. That is also when you should turn your manuscript over to a professional editor, who will find thirty-one typos, a sentence that makes no sense to anyone but you, and numerous mistakes in punctuation. Sadly, the editor will not find that one last spelling error that nobody noticed until after the book went to print.

A Cautionary Tale

If you are among those writers who claim to dislike this last crucial phase of the creative process, I hope this chapter has changed your opinion, and that now you, too, can see the satisfaction, even pleasure, that can come from maniacal editing. If, however, at any time in your editing future, you still find yourself weakening, and tempted to let the almost-right word suffice, my suggestion is to take a break, close your eyes, and reflect on this little story:

Once upon a time, ten years from now, you spy your own book on the shelf. You pull it down and crack open its dusty spine. Your attention is drawn to a single sentence amid pages of polished prose. You knew at the time of writing that something felt off, but you were tired. Oh, so very tired of reworking your language, of scrutinizing every sentence and word. *Who would notice?* you thought, as you called it quits. Would anyone even care?

Now open your eyes, because you have your answer. Once you have published a work, other writers may read it and claim, "I could write a better book than that!" Maybe they are right, maybe they are wrong, but one thing is certain—you don't want to be the one to make such a claim about your own book.

Happy Endings

There was a time when almost every middle-class family across America had a shelf occupied by a big, fat, doorstop of a hardcover dictionary. Households of the intellectually inclined favored the *Oxford English Dictionary* (OED), a bastion of conservatism in English usage. In my childhood home, where reading tastes ran more to murder mysteries and stories of grisly true crimes, we owned a Merriam-Webster's.

One summer when I was in graduate school, I earned extra income by house-slash-dog sitting for two married professors traveling on sabbatical. The woman taught German studies. The man was a musicologist. Their little wire-haired purebred was a dog-show reject thanks to his underbite. (The woman and I both agreed it only made him even more precious.) The most memorable feature of the professors' home was its study, which housed a ponderous dictionary situated on its own handcrafted bookstand. Carefully, I would turn the tome's membrane-thin pages piped with gold leaf. *Drip . . . milk . . . vacuum . . .* What place did these lowly words have in such a hallowed guide? The study also featured floor-to-ceiling bookshelves displaying texts in multiple languages, a cacophony of sheet music, and a curvaceous abstract sculpture that made me think of lovemaking or Dairy Queen, depending on my mood. So this was how real scholars lived! Such cross-cultural, multidisciplinary learnedness seemed like an impossibly far reach for a lowly graduate student with Merriam-Webster sensibilities.

Looking back, I would say that my house-slash-dog-sitting years coincided with the very beginning of the end of the Golden Age of Dictionaries. Now, thanks to the Internet, spell-check, and the purported decline of every younger generation that happens to come of age after ours, traditional reference guides are under constant threat of becoming anachronisms. To survive, they have become notably more competitive. ("Over 70,000 entries thoroughly revised and updated!") They have stretched beyond their core competencies, and innovated. ("Over 400 photographs and illustrations!") Sometimes, they have even resorted to undictionary-like practices to grow market share and maintain relevancy. The OED, for example, recently added the words "awesomesauce" and "Beer-O'clock" to its listings, which just feels desperate to me, like your newly divorced Uncle Harold, the collar of his Izod shirt turned up, his temples showing trace residue of Just for Men, out clubbing with a bunch of twentysomethings.

As a person who works in words, I find all this dictionary drama quite interesting. Lexicography matters—and really matters at English faculty gatherings where the Scotch flows freely —but maybe not so heatedly in our everyday lives. There is, however, one exception in which the principles and practices of a particular dictionary do affect directly the quality of our daily lives, or at least the quality of my daily life. By my definition, this particular reference is a sham, a scamy mockery of the foundational values of the first English dictionary, so named by a British philologist, poet, and university teacher in 1220 to help with Latin diction. In contrast, the purpose of this guide, as far as I can tell, is to take established words and phrases, and smear them with lowly connotations.

I am talking, of course, about the Urban Dictionary, an online resource started in 1999 by a freshman computer major at California Polytechnic State University. The owner's original intent was to create a parody of dictionary.com, but now this crowd-sourced online guide has gained a disturbing degree of legitimacy. It averages over 70 million impressions and almost 20 million unique readers, and anyone on Facebook or Gmail can make a submission. The upshot of such a populist guide is that now it is next to impossible to say certain things (including the word "upshot") without someone purposely taking it to mean something you do not want it to mean. As examples:

"Would you like a piece of toast?"
"Oh yeah, baybee, I'll take a piece of that toast any day."

"Wow. What a nice day. I think I'll go for a bicycle ride."
"Dayum! Did I ever go on a bicycle ride last night."

"Purple is my favorite color!"
"Man, when I smoke the purple I get so effed up."

Well, that is quite enough of that! Neither am I a prude, nor do I think when it comes to proper English usage I have an overdeveloped sensitivity chip. (Now, wouldn't that make for an interesting entry in the Urban Dictionary?) I believe in the freedom of speech (sometimes begrudgingly), so I could almost reconcile myself to the existence of a reference guide sourced primarily by gutter-mouths and pervs. After all, no one is making me go online and use it. My feelings changed considerably, though, once I learned that the Urban Dictionary had besmirched a phrase that I feel particularly protective about, as both a writer and a human being. In fact, this is a phrase I had enthusiastically proposed as the title of this very book.

Happy Endings!

My thinking at the time was this. The phrase has a positive connotation. For book browsers, its allure is the promise of a writing life that will turn out just fine. And, last but not least, the expression lends itself to a fun graphic!

"Uh, you know what that phrase means, right?" This was the response to my enthusiasm from my editor, my friends, the thirteen-year-old kid down the street . . .

Naïvely, I assured them that I did.

Even before it became an entry in the Urban Dictionary, the concept of happy endings had been compromised, not by street slangers who frequent massage parlors willing to throw in sexual favors for an extra fee, but by a group of people arguably in need of such a massage: literary snoots. Thanks to these snoots, the term *happy ending* in the writing realm has become associated, almost synonymous, with a story resolution that is trite and simplistic. But this association is what is trite and simplistic, a point that I have argued countless times with the imaginary snoots in my head.

> Me: "How can you discount the happy ending when plenty of works of literature—*Pride and Prejudice, Great Expectations, Lord of the Rings!*—have cheery conclusions?"
>
> Snoot to a fellow snoot: "Preston, did you hear something? There seems to be a bothersome buzzing in the room."

Despite being right about the legitimacy of the happy ending, not to mention the fact that I play both parts in this internal dialogue, I still manage to come out of it feeling like a petulant child. It is hard, really hard, to win an argument with snoots, especially those who look down their noses at any character more fortunate than Ethan Frome. Consequently, too many contemporary literary authors fear that their work will be cheapened, or that they will not be taken seriously as an artist and as a person, if they choose to have things to turn out well in their stories. And things only seem to be getting worse. Just look at the current boom in dystopian fiction, for example, a prevalence that also plays out in the manuscripts I am asked to read as an instructor for graduate-level creative writing programs, and at my own writer's center.

Zombies. Pandemics. Evil technologies that have taken over the world and destroyed civilization as we know it. Sometimes I wish a computer virus transmitted by the undead would wipe out every student manuscript set in a postapocalyptic universe. But of course such an attitude does not represent quality teaching, though that doesn't mean I don't make a good point.

To preempt any misunderstanding as to what I mean by a happy ending, I would like to clarify here that I am not talking about a story resolution that relies on an outside agent like a fairy godmother or the plot device of a *deus ex machina* to intervene and magically solve all the protagonist's problems. I also am not talking about contrivances, for example, attributing your narrator's problems to the spicy shrimp he indulged in the night before, which caused him to have a very bad dream. And now, thanks to the Urban Dictionary, I feel I should add here that I also am not talking about hand jobs.

To understand what I do mean by a happy ending, consider two of the essential components of creative writing—character and plot—and how they might interact toward an outcome that is justifiably both positive and literary. For the sake of expediency, let me distill these two components down to their essences. Character is emotion. Plot is motion. Your character's emotions set the plot in motion or, conversely, the plot inspires emotion that motivates the character to take action. It is this integration of character and plot—emotion and motion—that drives the narrative forward until it culminates in a crisis, or decisive moment, or point of no return. Should this situation resolve in a happy outcome? A tragic conclusion? An ambiguous ending? None of those choices is intrinsically superior, though literary snoots would have you believe otherwise. Instead, the best choice comes down to the answer to one overarching question: What is in service to your story?

Look at it this way. A narrative is inspired by a character who wants something of great value to her, whether that something is a quiet moment with a cup of tea, her brother's girlfriend, or to save her village from marauders. As the narrative progresses, she goes after what she wants and, depending on the confluence of emotion, motivation, and motion, just might get it, even without the help of a fairy godmother. It can happen, you know, in literature and in life.

Just as the snoots look down their noses at the happy ending in literature, the relevance of happiness in our creative lives is also discounted. Rather than being seen as a contributing factor to our success, happiness (meaning a state of well-being or joyfulness, lest there be any confusing alternative in the Urban Dictionary) is treated with suspicion or even mocked.

I went to dinner the other night with a woman who is a novelist and, admittedly, one of my most snooty friends. We had not hung out for quite a while, and she asked me what I was working on.

"I'm finishing a book about creativity and happiness," I told her. I went on to explain that happiness was a theme that had asserted itself more and more during the writing process. What had become clear to me as I worked on the book was that the relationship between the two—productivity and happiness—flows both ways. When we write more and write better, naturally we tend to be happier. But when we develop a greater sense of well-being through healthy writing practices and an improved perspective, we are also more likely to write more and write better.

"Creativity and happiness," my friend repeated in a mocking tone. "That does sound gloomy."

And just like that, I felt embarrassed for wasting my time on such trite subject matter. Now, if I had been writing about angst and the vital role that plays in the creative process, maybe that would have earned me some respect.

"Yeah, all this positive thinking is bringing me down," I joked. In truth, though I still had plenty of difficult writing days, I knew that I had been a lot happier (and less neurotic) working on this book than on my previous ones. I attributed this in large part to the fact that I was consciously applying what I was learning as I was writing; whereas before, happiness had never been a focus of my creative process. Yet, here I sat with my snooty friend, acting the traitor to my own book because I was too chicken to speak my truth. It was third grade all over again, a time when I had a best playmate, Diana, who spent part of the school year with her head in bandages after undergoing surgery to fix her protruding ears. Even without the bandages, Diana was not a popular girl, so when we were around our other classmates, I distanced myself from her. My betrayal was subtle. I never joined in the mean teasing, but I knew what I was doing then, just as I knew what I was doing now—failing to assert my loyalty so that no one would associate me with big ears.

The time had come to make amends to Diana, and to redeem myself for the sake of my own integrity. I clarified to my snooty friend that I was not suggesting people only write about happy things, or that writing should always be easy and fun. Rather, the book was intended to draw attention to the positive role that happiness can play in our creative lives. "Think about the Declaration of Independence," I said, believing that I had hit on just the right analogy. "One of the most important documents in the world states that we have three inalienable rights: life, liberty, and the pursuit of happiness. Happiness may not be a given like the other two," I added, "but why would we squander our right to pursue it?"

There! I had spoken up, and who could argue with the Declaration of Independence?

"I just don't think writers see happiness as a goal." My friend buttered her crusty roll. "It's not really the point of what we do."

I happened to be working on this chapter on my birthday when my ex-husband called to tell me that his mom had died. She was a lovely person, and I have always considered myself lucky to have had her as a mother-in-law. The news of her passing, not unexpected though sooner than predicted, evoked a kaleidoscope of memories. She had been a majorette in college, wore bright pink lipstick, and presided over story hour at the library where she worked. She never minded the chill of the ocean, drove extra miles to save a few cents, and always lit up at the sight of her granddaughters when we visited. Every Christmas, she exchanged handcrafted ornaments with the "girls," her sorority sisters from over sixty years ago.

A birthday is a natural opportunity to take stock of one's life, but when it coincides with the last day of life for someone with whom you have been close, it inspires you to take stock with more scrutiny. The loss of my former mother-in-law on the date of my birth seemed to compress time, accentuating the brevity of our years on this planet. The thought struck me that no matter who we are or where we start out in life, all of our stories end exactly the same way. This should not have been a shocker, but maybe because I had just been thinking about my upcoming birthday party, and writing about happy endings, I felt blindsided by this reality. Maybe the snoots were right, I thought, not about literature but about life. To contrive a plausible happy ending for our personal stories would indeed require the intervention of a fairy godmother or *deus ex machina*. But this reality also brought forth another truth, equally self-evident: The success of our own story is not determined by its ending, but rather by what we do in the time before we reach that inevitability.

Happiness can be an elusive goal, and while we have the inalienable right to pursue it, what often remains in doubt is whether we have the gumption and energy to do so. To cultivate a sense of well-being, and open ourselves up to joy, requires a commitment to positive practices. It can take a seismic shift of consciousness to own up to the fact that we matter, and so does our writing. It can take considerable courage to overcome doubts and fears in order to reap the rewards that come from asserting our voices and claiming our contributions to humanity. And all the while the snoots of this weary world—and of course the Urban Dictionary—are likely to mock our efforts.

"Oh, you're looking for a happy ending? That'll cost you twenty bucks."

In the face of these challenges, why should you seek happiness as a goal?

Because I am a writer, and determined to win an argument with the snoots in my head and at large, I will put forth here an answer rooted in those two essential components of creative writing: character and plot.

Character is emotion. Plot is motion. The integration of the two is what moves our narratives forward. In writing, we have the opportunity to choose our endings, but in life, the only choices we have are the ones that define us today, and tomorrow, and every day thereafter until we draw our last breath. Of course, we do not need to pursue happiness to write well. We do not need to cultivate a more optimistic outlook and adopt positive practices to succeed in any realm, or to get through an ordinary day. But as the author of our own narratives, I think the best choices in life, as in writing, come down to the answer to one overarching question: What is in service to our story?

I hope you choose happiness, because you just may get it. It can happen, you know, in literature and in life.

Acknowledgments

Once I finish work on a book, I could go around thanking and hugging everybody, but effective writing is all about selectivity, so I will limit myself here to listing those people who helped me directly in this effort, whether they knew it or not. First, thank you to my editor, Richard Pult at UPNE, whose email response to my book proposal was one of the best opening lines I have ever read —*I'm very pleased to tell you . . .*

A special thanks to the following people: Steve Cole, who takes such great care of his family; Deborah McKew, a creative lifeline for me and so many others; Nancy Fontaine, my breakfast brainstormer and website caregiver; Becky Joffrey, a force of inspiration; and Frances McManus, for her love and light. To my clubhouse friends and fellow writers—Lisa Barfield, Suzanne Coté-Curtiss, Mike Humphrey, Paula Nulty, and Marjorie Sa'adah —I want to publicly affirm that you guys are the best! And adorbz to a one.

I am also grateful to the following individuals who make me want to write, feed my love of teaching, and/or make me look smarter with their feedback and wisdom: Pam Broadley, Kendra Colburn, Lacey Colligan, Kwame Dawes, Chris Demers, Dan Deneen, Casey Dennis, Dixie Eastridge, Jennifer Falvey, Mike Fanizzi, Laura Foley, Ah-reum Han, Linda Hazard, Deborah Heimann, Alison Hine, Don Kollisch, Marjorie Matthews, Martha McLafferty, Jennifer Minotti, Sasha Mordecai, Geraldine North, Kristy O'Meara, Carl Small, Abby Tassel, Ed Ting, and Sheila Tanzer.

A manuscript is not a book, and to make that transformation takes a lot of work at the publishing house, which is often left unacknowledged because, well, because the author wrote the acknowledgments before that whole process began. But I have never been a writer afraid of last-minute "author alterations," so I would like to add here my thanks to the following people at University Press of New England for their talents in copyediting, design, production, marketing, publicity, and sales: Barbara Briggs, Eric Brooks, Michael Burton, Amanda Dupuis, Sara Evangelos, Katy Grabill, Andrew Lohse, Sherri Strickland, and Susan Sylvia.

My appreciation also extends to all the writers who have graced the workshops at my writer's center with their stories, insights, and support of one another. I also want to thank my workshop participants in the MALS program at Dartmouth College, at the Hartford (Vermont) Community Restorative Justice Center, the Comprehensive Women's Care Center at the VA Medical Center in White River Junction, and WISE, which supported nearly 1,000 victims of domestic violence in our community in the past fiscal year alone. I am lucky to sit in your circles. Thanks, as well, to the Vermont Studio Center and the Vermont Arts Council, whose generosity allowed me two weeks of focused writing time overlooking the ice floes of the Gihon River.

P.S. Direct marketing experts advise reserving one of your most important messages for the postscript because it draws more attention, and is often read first. With that in mind, I have included here a special acknowledgment to my partner, Helmut Baer, who is my heart, my head holder, my creative collaborator, and the most fun person I know. Thank you for always being there for me.

About the Author

In work and in life, author and teacher Joni B. Cole prefers a macro lens, seeking the extraordinary in the ordinary, the significance in everyday moments. Her book *Toxic Feedback: Helping Writers Survive and Thrive* is "strongly recommended" for students and teachers by *Library Journal*. ("I can't imagine a better guide to [writing's] rewards and perils than this fine book," *American Book Review*.) She is the author of the personal essay collection *Another Bad-Dog Book: Essays on Life, Love, and Neurotic Human Behavior* ("riotously funny and outrageously honest," Gina Barreca). Joni is also the creator of the three-volume This Day book series that reveals the reality of a day in the life of hundreds of women across America and from all walks of life ("fascinating and eye-opening," *Publisher's Weekly*). She founded the Writer's Center of White River Junction, Vermont, serves on the faculty of the New Hampshire Institute of Art, and teaches writing workshops at the Master of Arts in Liberal Studies program at Dartmouth College. Joni also leads expressive writing workshops for a variety of educational and social services programs. She has been nominated for a Pushcart Prize and a United States Artists Fellowship, and is a frequent teacher and speaker at conferences around the country. Joni lives in Vermont and has two daughters. For more information, visit www.jonibcole.com.